PAY IT FORWARD

Infusing Unconditional Love Into Business

PAY IT FORWARD

Infusing Unconditional Love Into Business

JORDI RICART

Watch Alan, John, and Jordi share the Pay It Forward story.

DEDICATION

Back in November 2023, Michael Harth (Alan Lazowski's business partner and Head of People and Culture at LAZ Parking) called me to mention that my *Pay It Forward* story had inspired him and the LAZ Management Team. They decided to use "Pay It Forward" as a theme for LAZ Parking in 2024. He asked me to join their annual reunion to tell my story and bring my "book." I didn't yet have a book! I just had a bunch of papers with a preliminary draft. If it had not been for Michael, I'm not sure this book would have ever been published! Michael, I thank you from the bottom of my heart!!!

I am not a professional writer and I'm not native to the English language, so I needed help! And once again, the Universe provided me with the help I needed. This book would not have the depth and energy that it has if it wasn't for an angel named Deanna. It's been one of the most incredible experiences to be able to open my heart and be vulnerable with a total stranger. We ended up both crying many times, sharing, and getting deep together. Thank you so much, Deanna, for putting all my thoughts, emotions, and energy into words.

The first draft that I gave to Alan for his birthday had another angel that helped me clean it up and organize. Brooke, thank you for believing so strongly in the message and for helping me with that first draft.

John Temerian! This book would not exist without you! You and me — we are this book. We went through so much together, and we both decided to support each other and grow together! I love you, my brother! Thank you for your Unconditional optimism, support, and love!

Jim Goetz, Thank you for believing in John and me! and always pushing us to Dream bigger! Having you as a partner and mentor has been a Dream!

Brother Gerard Subirats! Thank you for giving me the opportunity to come to Miami to support you! Thank you for believing in me! I will be forever grateful! T'estimo!

Ana and Hershel, CURATED would probably not exist if it wasn't for you. You both have been there since day one supporting John, CURATED, and me unconditionally. I love you!

The whole CURATED team: Ana, Hershel, Ryan, Katya, Nandina, Miguel, Ernesto, Hooper, Tyler, Ruben, Barton, Derian, Stephen, Sergio, Rebeca, Nick, Luiz, Ross, Chris, Elijah, Gavin, Juliana, Sean, Gabriel, Scott, and many others … You guys are rockstars! Thank you for opening your hearts and embracing the Culture that we built all together. Be proud of what we have created — it is very special.

To all the clients, vendors, and community that supported us, THANK YOU! But especially to those two bankers who believed in us when nobody did and gave us the first opportunity, Herve and Augusto! Thank you!

To my first boss, Jose Miguel. The one that made me cry many times. The toughest boss I have ever had. You taught me so much about business. How a company works, how it's structured, its operations, accounting, creating great reporting, and so much more! And you also taught me what I didn't want to have in my future company. Thank you, Jose Miguel, for teaching me the best you knew how and helping me to be a better business manager.

To my incredible Coaches and friends Patty and Monica for guiding me on a 4-year journey to connect with my soul, discover who I really am, and help me be the best version of myself.

To my Mom and Dad for always being my number one supporters and teaching me values and educating me with a super open-mind mentality. Us estimo!

To my daughters, Emma and Gala. I hope that one day you can read this book and feel proud of your dad.

To the love of my life, my wife, Andrea. My biggest supporter. Without her, I wouldn't be able to do half of the things I do in my life. She is the rock that keeps everything in place and gives me the time and space to try to make an impact on the world. I love you, Andrea.

And finally, to Alan. You changed my life, and by changing mine, you changed many other people's lives. Thank you for helping me see life from another perspective, one where love is in the center. Once I told you, "They are bad people," and immediately you answered, "That's the difference between you and me, I believe that everyone is a good person." I have to accept that that comment hurt me but you were so right. Thanks to you, I realized that deep inside everyone wants to be a good person but many times they just don't know how. And as you say, they need a second chance and someone that believes in them more than themselves. Thank you for sharing so much my wisdom with me. I will forever try to share this wisdom with as many people as possible.

All quotations in this book are
attributed to Alan Lazowski,
unless otherwise specified.

Pay it forward to someone else by scanning this code!

CONTENTS

FOREWORD

by Alan Lazowski

We all have an opportunity to be a force for good to make our world a better place and help others in need.

"Paying It Forward" is an age-old gift that can be described as someone doing a good deed for another person without expecting anything in return. The hope is that the recipient of kindness will in turn do something good for someone else. This act of goodness and kindness can and will create a ripple effect of kindness and generosity. These uplifting outcomes will spread positive actions to other individuals and to our greater communities and beyond.

The idea is: Rather than repay a favor directly to the person who helped you, you "Pay It Forward" by helping someone else. This action can happen in small everyday situations — like buying a coffee for someone in line behind you or in a more significant way like going out of your way to help someone in need.

My own personal family history and story has led me to a path of paying it forward.

Both my parents are Holocaust survivors, and at 11 years of age my dad, Rabbi Philip Lazowski, was saved in a selection line facing death. The person who saved him was a beautiful woman who he had never met before. She risked her life and her two daughters' lives (ages 7 and 5) to save a little boy that she had never met before.

My Dad had only met this woman briefly, and unfortunately his mother, two brothers, and a sister were killed. He survived by living in the woods of Poland for 2 years with his Father and brother. Eventually, my Dad made it to the United States, and 12 years later at the age of 23 years old, as fate would have it, he found the beautiful woman that saved his life! He married her oldest daughter, my mother Ruth, who was in the Nazi selection line with my Dad when they were children. My Dad became one of the greatest spiritual leaders in Connecticut with my mom by his side. And they both have paid forward acts of goodness and kindness to thousands of people. Their story is written in two books *Faith & Destiny* by Philip Lazowski and *Into the Forest* by Rebecca Frankel.

In 1981, I was fortunate to be able to start a small parking business with my lifelong friends. Today, LAZ Parking is one of the largest parking companies in the United States with over 15,000 amazing family members!!

At LAZ, we believe in Conscious Capitalism, elevating humanity through business. We believe that business should be and can be a force for good.

We often say we are only as good as the people we have working with us. We believe that we must take care of all our stakeholders, our employees, our vendors, the communities we serve, and our environment. Our purpose and mission at LAZ is to "Create Opportunities for our Employees and Value for our Clients."

Meeting Jordi Ricart and John Temerian, and being able to help them on their journey, has been one of the great gifts of my lifetime. Watching them achieve success and "Pay It Forward" is a dream come true!!

Thank you, Jordi, for all your love and kindness. And congratulations on writing such an amazing book, which will influence the world.

With Love and Gratitude,

Alan Lazowski

INTRODUCTION

September 2, 2015. 6:00 pm. I found myself sitting alone at my desk in a warehouse surrounded by high-end cars in Miami, Florida, seeing my life dreams slip away from me. The path ahead was daunting and uncertain.

At 32 years old, I had two college degrees from a university in my native country, Spain. And I had worked tirelessly. But now, I faced a failed business, empty bank accounts, and the worry of how to pay rent and my mounting immigration attorney fees.

Simply put, the future looked bleak.

At the time, I was co-leading one of the largest luxury and exotic car rental agencies in the country, Lou La Vie, in Miami, Florida, with my business partner, John Temerian. John is the third generation of his family working in the realm of European blue chip automobiles. He's basically an encyclopedia about 70s, 80s, and 90s Lamborghinis and Ferraris. The exact opposite, I was an immigrant without a history of luxury car knowledge who had been in the US for two years. And so far, business had been going pretty well — until it wasn't. About 70% of our clientele were Brazilians visiting Miami. So when Brazil went into a recession and their currency devalued, we lost 70% of our business within only 3 months! Any money we had went to pay our employees, our car loans, and the rent on our warehouse. For 6 months, John and I didn't even take a salary. Month after month, we thought each one would be our last day in business. But something always happened that kept us afloat.

By the time September arrived, John had pawned his Rolex watch just to be able to pay his rent.

Meanwhile, I had only $150 in my bank account.

So now here I was, sitting alone at my desk in our warehouse surrounded by our high-end cars and beautiful artwork. And I thought, *This is it! My dream is over. I have to return to Spain.* But, I didn't even have enough money for a plane ticket. My life in the US was hanging by a thread.

As I began mentally compiling a list of friends and family I could ask for financial assistance, fate intervened in the form of a phone call.

"Hello, Jordi! It's Alan!"

It was Alan Lazowski, the founder of LAZ Parking, the largest parking company in the United States with $2 billion in revenues under management and over 15,000 employees.

John and I met Alan in 2014 by accident. Lou La Vie had hosted one of the largest Art Basel events in Miami. Alan was in town from Connecticut on a business trip and had heard about the event through a friend. He decided to show up at our showroom the next day. The event was amazing — over 1,000 people were there. Art was everywhere. DJs were spinning music. People were mingling. Mr Brainwash was live-painting a Maserati that we owned. The vibe was exciting. Then, out of nowhere, this guy wearing shorts and flip-flops walked in screaming, "Wooooowww, what is this all about? This is crazy!"

It was Alan.

After that visit to our showroom, Alan took our phone numbers and started calling us at night and meeting us for dinner every time he was in Miami for business. He started mentoring us! At first, I hadn't fully understood why he wanted to keep in touch with us. We had nothing to offer him. We were two young entrepreneurs struggling to keep our almost bankrupt business afloat. The future seemed uncertain. Meanwhile, Alan was the exact opposite — an incredibly successful entrepreneur who, at the time, had even been appointed by President Barack Obama to lead the Holocaust Memorial Museum in Washington, D.C.

Now, here he was calling me during one of the darkest, most desperate-feeling moments of my life. With his characteristic enthusiasm, Alan exclaimed,

"Hey Jordi, I miss you! I'm in Miami for the National Parking Association Convention. If you and John are free in 20 minutes, let's grab dinner."

I agreed to go and called John to share our invite.

Thirty minutes later, we found ourselves seated at Mandolin Restaurant, engaged in conversation with this remarkable individual. As our conversation unfolded, Alan, as usual, inquired about our business with Lou La Vie. We shared how things weren't going well. And then, Alan asked, "What about the old cars you buy and sell? Have you pursued more deals?"

Alan was referencing a side hustle John and I had started doing. In months prior, I'd seen John buying affordable vintage cars for himself, driving them for a while, and then selling them for a profit. One day, I asked him if we could do this as a business, and he said, "Yes, but we don't have the money." That very day, I started raising money through friends. So, we began buying and selling cars for $50,000 to $150,000, generating good profits and sharing it with our investors. In fact, at this point, these deals had become our sole means of survival since we hadn't received a paycheck in months.

When Alan asked about these cars, John was filled with excitement about one he'd found. He proclaimed, "I've actually found 'the deal!' We'll be rich! We can buy this car for $800,000 and sell it for $1 million to $1.1 million."

John had found a Lamborghini Miura S — I didn't even know what that was — that someone was selling on eBay and was just sitting in their shed loft undrivable but in solid condition.

I was embarrassed to even bring up this deal to Alan. We had practically no money to our names. I thought John was too optimistic, his head living in the clouds.

So, I responded pessimistically to Alan, saying, "That sounds great, but I'll never be able to raise $800,000 for a car within two weeks. We need to submit a $50,000 deposit by the end of this week, and we have nothing in our bank account."

Alan burst into laughter.

Undeterred, John exclaimed, "You'll see — we'll make it happen!" Alan kept laughing and said, "You guys are crazy!"

I said, "Yeah, John is crazy!"

Alan looked at me and declared, "You are as crazy as him because you follow him, but I love it!"

Amidst the laughter, Alan pulled something out of his bag and started writing something I couldn't see. Suddenly he looked at me and said, "Jordi, you're the money guy, right?" I nodded in confirmation. He continued, "So, here you have $50,000 for your deposit. Tomorrow, make the deposit, and within the next two weeks, raise the remaining $750,000. Once you accomplish that, John will sell the car for $1,100,000."

I couldn't believe what was transpiring before my eyes. A person we had met only a few times — someone with whom we had sporadic phone conversations — was offering us $50,000 without any formal contract.

Overwhelmed, I objected, "Alan, I won't be able to raise this money. You'll lose your deposit."

Alan locked eyes with me and replied, "I believe in you! You will raise the money."

John and I sat there, tears streaming down our faces, overcome with emotions we couldn't fully process. *What should we do? Should we accept the check? What if we couldn't raise the money? What if we couldn't sell this $800,000 car?* After all, we had never undertaken a transaction of such magnitude before.

As we stared at the check, our tear-filled eyes gradually focused, and Alan asked, "Have you read the check?"

In unison, we replied, "Yes."

Alan urged us, "Read it again."

So, we looked again and saw a message in the check's Memo section. Alan had written, "PAY IT FORWARD." We were confused — and I especially was. At the time, my English wasn't as strong as it is now. I didn't know what he meant.

Alan asked, "Do you guys know the difference between 'pay it back' and 'pay it forward?'" We shook our heads.

Alan enlightened us, "When you have the opportunity to help someone, you do it! I want you guys to do for other people what I did for you today.

I want you guys to help your employees, your clients, your vendors, and anyone you can."

In that moment of kindness, Alan changed our lives forever.

But, we didn't yet realize the significance of the lesson we had just learned. We were oblivious to the chain of events that would unfold in the months and years to come.

As we left the restaurant that evening — our hearts filled with gratitude and a newfound hope — we embarked on a journey. And so began my mentorship with the amazing Alan Lazowski.

And our lives would never be the same!

When I first entered the business world, I approached leadership from a place of negativity and fear. My first jobs in Spain had groomed this culture in me. Business wasn't personal — it was business. And you had to lead with a mindset of "kill or be killed" in order to survive.

After meeting Alan, my whole perspective on business changed. Through my years of mentorship from him, I've learned firsthand that in order to truly be successful, you have to lead with unconditional love, ethics, and moral excellence. You have to use your heart and help others as much as possible. By doing so, only then can you, your business, and the world around you truly thrive.

I am not a professional writer. I'm simply an entrepreneur who had the privilege of crossing paths with someone who changed my life, Alan Lazowski.

After Alan gave us that $50,000, he did so much more than enable us to do a profitable transaction. He provided an opportunity for me to experience how to be a better person. How to interact with people, approach tasks, and navigate challenges not from the mind or from aggression — but from the heart.

During the first meetings I had with Alan, he used to ask me a lot about myself, especially about my thoughts and my life back in Spain. Almost every night, he called me at around 10 pm, and we'd spend hours on the phone talking about business and life. Many times, Alan used to suggest an idea and I used to answer, "That's impossible, Alan." I remember him telling me that anything is possible in life and to never give up. Many, many times, he gave me the example of his family and their amazing story surviving the Holocaust.

As soon as I found my mentorship with Alan, I began taking notes of everything he told me, shared with me, inspired in me. These were life-changing lessons that I hadn't learned anywhere else — not in my university studies or any books I read.

Eventually, the insights I gained were too valuable to keep to myself. So I committed to writing this book so that I could share these newfound perspectives with others.

I began the writing process in 2014. And the content has been evolving since. After each meeting with Alan, I found myself reflecting — revising the text, adding new insights, and deleting old ones. And with every new day of Alan's mentorship, more and more, the way I saw the world was changing. And then, following a powerful weekend with Alan during an important negotiation for one of our projects, I left the event finally ready to share all I have learned and the way I now see the world.

And in that moment, Pay It Forward was born to showcase a different approach to business and to energize entrepreneurs with a better way to succeed through unconditional love.

I've also written this book as a tribute to Alan — business mogul, philanthropist, and founder of LAZ Parking.

Alan started LAZ in 1981 while he was in college as a valet parking company. He and his two partners (all of them are childhood best friends) have grown the company to be worth over a billion dollars. And Alan is known for his people-first leadership style, unconditional kindness, and steadfast tenacity. LAZ Parking's success is greatly due to this leadership style, which he and his partners have infused within the company's culture.

After a year mentoring us, Alan helped us pursue an ambitious dream with that $50,000 check, believing in our capability more than I did in that moment. And we not only were able to buy that car within two weeks — we sold it for over $1.2 million, even more money than we anticipated, and were able to pay Alan back. After that deal's success, Alan shared that he believed we were onto something big with these vintage car deals. He offered to help us structure and grow the business, and CURATED was born.

Today, I am beyond fortunate to call him a mentor, partner, friend, and one of the most special people in my life. Alan transformed the way I look at people, business, and life. He taught me the secret of happiness: to lead with love.

Years before meeting him — while still living in Barcelona — I began contemplating happiness often. I earnestly wanted to ascertain the key to happiness, and so I started reading books and talking to people studying the concept. Even though I learned about happiness, I never discovered anything new or life-altering. So, I maintained my belief that money had a significant correlation with happiness and that driving a nice car or having a nice house would lead to this goal. Within this paradigm, and as I have advanced in my career, I have been very successful. I've established and grown some businesses, earned good money, and accomplished most of the goals I set for myself when I was a student.

However, it took meeting Alan for me to truly understand that love — not material gain — is the key to happiness.

During this time, I've also begun a personal journey of self-improvement. I now have a mindset coach and a spiritual coach. I've been studying hypnosis, meditation, and breathwork. And I have truly transformed the way I see the world and the role love plays within it. From this personal growth, I have come to know that the secret of happiness is singular: dedicate your life to helping others. Create opportunities for people, support them, and bask in the delight of seeing them grow.

So, the goal of this book is to demonstrate that you can, in the words of Alan, "Elevate humanity through business." Rather than see business as a tool to make money, we can use business as an instrument to improve the quality of life for people and the communities they live in. This approach is both #TheLazWay and the #PayItForward mentality.

My goal is to create a ripple effect of kindness, empathy, and happiness.

I will note: Everything I share in this book takes a fair amount of time and practice to integrate in your daily life. It took me years, but the results are unbelievable.

To help you, I'm sharing advice that I've learned from Alan over the years. Each chapter opens with a quote directly from Alan and then explores my experience with this perspective. I also end each chapter with a takeaway for you by prompting you with two tools: 1) hypnosis meditation and 2) journal exploration.

The reason for these prompts is to help you explore how to apply what you're learning. So, I want to make everything tangible for you by having you reflect on each chapter's guidance and Alan's wisdom.

Why hypnosis meditations?

Hypnosis and meditation are ways to rewire our

brains. The way our thinking patterns go is this: First, we have a thought. Then, this thought creates an emotion and the emotion will create action and behavior. Ninety-five percent of our cognition lives in our subconscious. So, we're typically not even aware of all the thoughts we have and how past experiences have affected us. To be able to change the way we think, we need to rewire our brain and start having new thoughts with positive emotions attached to them. By doing so, we can help change the way we act! For this reason, I wanted to create this tool to help you succeed when applying this book's principles.

And the same thinking goes with the journal prompts. Writing out how we feel can greatly boost our wellbeing. You can even help reduce anxiety and boost your immune system by writing your feelings. Plus, it's a great way to process information that you're learning. So, I encourage you to have an honest connection with yourself and think about how you are leading your business and life. Go deep on these journal prompts and find out who you are today. They will help you define the person you want to be 5 years from now! A complete new person, fulfilled and leading with love.

And track your growth along your Pay It Forward journey!

Finally, I feel compelled to apologize to those who met the first version of me and suffered because of me.

I came to Miami from Barcelona as a single man with a broken heart and broken engagement. I had a failed business relationship with a partner who took complete advantage of me. Today, I own a company with over $100M in revenue with my business partner, John, who has become my best friend. Our other partners are Alan and Jim Goetz, a venture capitalist and the former CEO of Sequoia Capital (known for deals like Whatsapp and as the number one tech investor in the world for five years).[1] And all of this started because my dear childhood friend, Gerard Subirats, invited me to come help him

---

1   Forbes Midas list (top venture capitalists) ranked Jim Goetz as the #1 investor from 2013 to 2017.

in his car rental business in Miami, which I ended up selling to Lou La Vie. Had he never connected with me, perhaps I'd never even be here sharing this book with you!

The Jordi of 2015 — who sat in the dark warehouse room and couldn't even afford to buy a plane ticket back to Spain — would never believe where my life would take me today. I'm married and have two beautiful daughters that didn't exist when I started drafting this book. And my life — personally and professionally — is one of love, which I'm incredibly thankful for.

All of this would not have been possible without the support of John, Alan, Jim, Gerard, and my wonderful wife, Andrea. I'm incredibly grateful.

1

EMBRACE POSITIVE THINKING

"What does it take to make somebody's day?"

Sunday night. The end of the weekend, and already, I could feel anxiety brewing in my stomach. Every week, I went through this ritual as I anticipated work on Monday. Like I was preparing myself to go to war.

At the time, I was working in a global company in Barcelona, Spain, as the operations manager. Early in my career, I was only 24 years old, bright faced and eager to begin my business journey. So, I was ready to show up to work and face the day, and pour myself into my responsibilities. As one of the youngest team members, I was managing a group of mostly women over 10 years my age. I was the rookie who felt I had a lot to prove to show my worth and value as an employee. As a manager. As an entrepreneur.

And I was ready for the challenge.

Each Sunday night, however, I was met with the same impending doom: Monday. And each weekend, my stomach ached.

By morning, I had to be ready to bear a full week of my boss. Although he was a shrewd businessman, he often had a negative attitude and led the company through fear. So, every week I had to endure him relentlessly pushing me, talking down to me, and yelling at me or someone on my team. The environment was stressful, deflating, and mentally and spiritually draining. Although at the time, I couldn't fully recognize just how heavy this working situation was. To me, it was the only post-university work environment I'd known. So rather than complain, I had to suck it up and fit in.

After all, business was business. And since my

dream was to be an entrepreneur, I felt I had no choice but to endure.

Growing up in Spain during the early 2000s, dreaming to be an entrepreneur wasn't the norm. A survey conducted in Spain revealed that most young adults' professional goal was to become public servants who worked from 8 am to 3 pm Although the pay wasn't amazing, the hours and lifestyle were relatively easy.

I, however, had a different vision for my life.

Raised in a middle-class family, I dreamed of being an entrepreneur. When I was a teenager, my father started his own business, so entrepreneurship was normalized for me. I saw firsthand that you could be your own boss and find your career outside of a government environment. Despite the struggles I saw my father have at times — and how this affected my family in moments — overall, my family was happy. And I knew I wanted the same for my life, and more. I knew business was my destiny.

So, I dreamed bigger.

In university, I studied dual degrees of Business

Administration and Law with visions to be either the general manager of a large company or a business owner. My goal? Be super successful. Really, my long-term dreams were quite simple: Make good money. Drive a nice car. And be able to buy whatever I wanted at a restaurant without worrying how much anything cost.

I was ready to work hard for that lifestyle.

To achieve that goal, I wanted to learn as much as I could from the business world. I always told myself that I was not going to prioritize making money until I was 30 years old. Until then, all I wanted to focus on was on getting business experience. As soon as I felt I was not learning more in operations, I wanted to work on my sales experience. So, I joined a company as a Sales Manager. A couple years later, I joined a company as a Sales Director. And all these experiences were in different industries.

My only goal was to acquire as much business experience as I could. I was willing to do anything to be successful one day in the future and achieve the life I envisioned. Even if that vision meant enduring an oppressive work environment.

And so, back in my role as Operations Manager, Monday morning arrived.

Helmet on, proverbially and literally, I hopped on my motorcycle and drove to the office. Ten minutes late thanks to a traffic accident, I knew my tardiness wouldn't bode well. So, I stood in front of the building and took a deep breath. Bracing myself with my emotional armor, I gave a weary and desperately optimistic, *Let's gooooo!* And walked through the large doors. Each step sealing the day's fate as I heard the oppressive security check-in of two large doors locking me inside.

Instantly, I was met with my boss's disapproving expression. His face stern and grumbly.

"Hello, Jordi," he tersely said.

"Hello! Good morning," I replied with a big smile.

"You are 10 minutes late." His eyes sharpened.

My smile sank to my gut. I looked around. My coworkers already had their heads down with miserable expressions. You could feel the tension.

And it was only Monday morning.

Here we go again…and again…and again…

At some point, if you're beaten down enough, you learn to normalize the behavior. And, you learn to mimic the behaviors of exactly what oppressed you.

Once I came to the United States in December 2012 to pursue my entrepreneurial dreams, I brought this mindset and behavior with me. I knew I was becoming the entrepreneur I needed to be to fulfill my path to business success.

Since I was groomed in business within a work environment based on fear, that's how I ended up managing others. Though I'm generally a happy, positive person, I became terse. I yelled. I had strict expectations. I had little room for incompetence, tardiness. When employees "messed up," I fired them. I felt I was ridding the company of weak links that would improve our efficiency. And I was proud of the fact that employees often didn't last under my management. I considered my difficult and "high expectations" the traits of a real leader.

Little did I realize how wrong I was.

Be Optimistic — and Share it With Others

Before I came to the US, I realized that many of my friends were expecting me to fail in business.

It wasn't their fault.

In Spain at the time, we didn't have a culture that looked at business people as someone to aspire to. A general opinion existed that if a business owner was rich, it wasn't because they had good intentions. *They had to be taking advantage of their employees.* If they drove a Ferrari, people thought, *Oh, he's stealing from his employees or did something illegal.* Surely, they couldn't simply be successful in business.

Plus, humans are wired for negativity. We'll inherently dwell in the negative more strongly than we do on the positive and make decisions from this mindset. This negativity bias is a way we evolved our survival instinct — the fight or flight mode.[1]

So, even though I have always been a relatively positive and smiley person (Even one of my history professors would say, "Jordi — the man who is always smiling."), I've not always been this person in the business world.

Growing up, we had enough money to get by but certainly were not rich and didn't have a big savings. While my father had his business, he had moments of financial ups and downs. And my parents were always very open about our finances and involved us in conversations. So, I became keenly aware of money. This perspective as a kid influenced who I became as an adult, and I developed an insecurity around money, so much so that I often became risk averse in business decisions. Rather than pay attention to what could go right, I focused more on what could go wrong in a situation. I became fixated on finding the holes. So, that's where I put my energy — into those gaps.

By doing so, however, I failed to focus on the opportunities before me and the abundance that optimism can offer. In hindsight, I missed so many moments that could've been wonderful if only I'd removed my skepticism and negative thinking.

At some point in Spain, I became aware of the fact that I had to leave Barcelona and go somewhere else where I could accomplish my dreams. I knew I needed to surround myself with people who were better than me, who would challenge me and invigorate me. That is the only way to achieve big things in life: Push yourself out of your comfort zone and believe in yourself.

And it's this positivity and optimism mindset that I found in Alan.

During my years at university, I became addicted to self-improvement books. In hundreds of books I read, "You attract what you think." I had always been a big believer of this quote but wasn't convinced it was 100% possible. When I met Alan, I saw for the first time a human being applying this philosophy at its largest exponent.

The first time I visited Alan's home in Nantucket, he picked us up at the airport beaming with excitement.

He had invited a group of 10 young professionals in our 30s — my business partner John and I included — to discuss launching a new business venture. When we got into his car, Alan switched the radio on and

"Lovely Day" started to play, followed by song after song related to happiness. That afternoon, we got into the swimming pools and Alan again blasted "Lovely Day." In fact, he played that song all weekend. And, all weekend I observed in detail how Alan surrounds himself with elements of positivity. He was the living, breathing realization of this concept I'd read about in countless books — infused into his M.O.

Alan was attracting positivity by living it, and by living it, he was generating more.

Throughout the weekend, Alan was continually telling us how happy and honored he was to be spending that time with us. How excited he was to work on the project together. By doing so, he was making us feel appreciated, heard, and inspired. He took his time fostering a weekend of fun and smiles while he showed all of us how far we could go with the project — how much we could all learn and earn. His optimistic enthusiasm was alluring and convincing, and completely contagious.

To Alan, the whole notion of optimism is about never, ever giving up. He's always saying, "Anything is possible — don't limit yourself!"

He believes that, every day, everyone has choices they can make. *Will this decision work? Will it not work? Should I do this? Should I not?* We go back and forth with this thinking. And we really don't know how something will pan out until we try it — yet, so many of us make this decision ahead of time. We formulate an opinion in our head that often isn't based in reality and decide not to pursue opportunities. Instead, we let our fears and our negativity make the decision.

By doing so, we limit our possibilities.

Optimism, however, can awaken potential. Studies show that people who are optimistic are more goal oriented. And they also tend to live longer, healthier lives. In the workplace, optimistic employees are 103% more inspired to give their best effort.[2]

And I've directly seen these results in action.

That moment when John and I were thinking of buying our first big vintage car (the Lamborghini Miura S) to sell together — and I was very skeptical that we could make it work — John was the exact opposite. The eternal optimist, John saw only the opportunity in our lap. And he shared this optimism and enthusiasm with Alan when we were having dinner with him. Rather than lean into the skepticism that was more natural for me, John only looked at the potential.

And this optimism played a large role in Alan's decision to write that $50,000 and help us with no guarantee that he would even get that money back.

Alan had a choice that day. And greatly because of John optimistically and wholeheartedly believing in the potential, Alan chose to pay it forward.

And he forever changed our lives.

Start the Day With a Smile and a Hug

The first day I visited the LAZ Parking headquarters with Alan, I was blown away.

At this point, CURATED was relatively new. While we were on the path toward creating a successful company, we weren't the force we were to become. And I certainly wasn't yet used to leading a company from a place of positivity every day.

Walking into LAZ Parking was like living a scene out of a movie! Alan was loudly greeting everyone, "Gooood morning!!" with a huge smile on his face. He was giving people hugs. He was telling employees how much he loved them.

In fact, everyone at LAZ Parking hugs one another — it's one of the key ways LAZ employees treat one another. Executives share a LAZ Hug with assistants. Colleagues share a LAZ Hug with teammates. Leaders LAZ Hug vendors. And they do so with a genuine, caring embrace for the other person's happiness.

In that first moment, I thought Alan was crazy! *What business owner tells his employees he loves them and hugs them?*

Here was a billion-dollar company with over 15,000 employees with their own hug! It's astounding — and effective.

Years later, I saw this behavior at a company-wide event LAZ invited me to speak at. Everyone who showed up was greeting each other with huge, excited hugs and smiles. And I mean, everyone was hugging! I'd never seen such warmth and excitement among hundreds of employees before. The energy was invigorating and contagious.

I've come to learn that this behavior isn't isolated moments. Every day of Alan's life, personally and professionally, he treats people this way. He leads the day with a smile — and offers that gesture to everyone he meets and works with. No matter if you're a janitor, clerk, senior executive, car attendant, Alan greets you with a smile and hug. I have observed Alan giving thousands of LAZ Hugs with his big smile, and it's incredible to see people's reactions. I've never seen anyone that appeared uncomfortable. Instead, I've observed the opposite! Alan's positivity and human connection has set a tone of warmth, openness, and conversation. Because to Alan, this behavior is just part of being a good human. And being a good human is the only way to do business.

Pause for a moment: Think about the impact a basic smile and a hug has on people in your life. On family members. On colleagues at work. On employees.

A pure smile accompanied by a friendly, "Good morning," can significantly impact your entire workplace atmosphere. This positivity raises the whole team's energy and vibration. In fact, the simple act of smiling fosters a positive emotional state. The brain releases dopamine and serotonin, our feel-good hormones. Smiling can also help reduce stress and lower blood pressure. Your immune system can even get a boost from a smile. Plus, smiles are contagious.[3] Similarly, hugs encourage the release of oxytocin and a breadth of positive effects on a person's wellbeing.[4]

And happier employees are more productive, fulfilled employees. One study found that 65% of employees believe that being treated respectfully is the most important driver of job satisfaction.[5]

Can you imagine a world where everybody wakes up in the morning with a smile? Where everybody seeks opportunities to help others while going through their daily routines?

So, leading with a smile and a hug can do more than simply be a nice gesture — you can genuinely and positively impact employees' quality of life. You authentically show that you respect them.

And ultimately, you foster a company culture that drives lasting loyalty and success.

Dream Big — Believe in Yourself

Before meeting Alan, I always thought that I was dreaming big. My colleagues and bosses told me that I would go far in business because I had grand-big dreams and a tenacious, dedicated work ethic. I worked hard. However, when I met Alan, I came to learn that my dreams were not big enough.

One day, I presented Alan with a business plan for a potential business venture. He went to the bottom line of the Profit and Loss statement, looked at me, and said, "I don't understand why you want to invest your time in this business."

I was shocked by his reply and didn't know what to say. I answered, "Because there's a potential $500,000 to be made at the end of the year."

Alan looked at me and said, "I think we should forget about this business and look for another one where investing the same amount of time has the potential to make $3M or more per year."

His response was eye opening — and one of the best lessons I ever learned.

At the time, $500,000 was a huge amount of money and more than anything I'd ever had. So that dream felt big to me! But, I was viewing my success with blinders on. I could only see a narrow field ahead of me. At that moment, Alan believed I had the potential to do more than what I even saw for myself. Through his optimism, he believed in me more than I did.

And I realized that my self-limiting thoughts were a direct response to my life experiences — and the choices I was making for myself.

Since that moment, I've gone on to co-lead a thriving, million-dollar business that continues to unfold new opportunities in my life. And I attribute much of this success to learning how to dream big, be optimistic, and believe in my potential.

In hindsight, my time as Operations Manager was one of the best things that could happen to me. While the environment had its ups and downs,

I learned a lot. I gained vast knowledge about the business world and the intricacies you must address to keep a company operational and thriving.

I also ended up learning who I naturally am as a businessperson — and that negativity isn't something I thrive in. In order to be the best version of myself, I had to overcome my fears and lead from a place of positivity. By doing so, my opportunities become limitless.

So, dear reader, even if your dreams seem big at the moment, remember: You have so much more potential than you may think.

Anything is possible in life! Why not embrace positivity — and dream even bigger?

HYPNOSIS MEDITATION

Believe, Behave, Become!

Scan this QR code for a guided hypnosis meditation. This meditation will help you connect your brain with your heart, allowing you to fully experience this chapter's emotions. By doing so, you can embrace its concepts and transform your behavior to align with the person you aspire to become!

JOURNALING

Do you start your day with a smile?

What do you do when you enter your office in the morning? What could you do differently?

What impact do you think that could have on other people?

In what ways can you better foster positivity for others and encourage employees to believe in themselves?

2

TALK TO EVERYBODY, AND LISTEN

> *"Talk to everybody —*
> *you never know who you*
> *are talking to."*

Growing up, I was a shy kid who was very introverted and had to exert incredible effort to meet (and later network with) people. Part of my shyness came from the fact that my family moved frequently, and I changed schools due to my father's job seven or eight times. And each change meant I had to endure an uncomfortable first day at my new school.

Typically, my first encounters with a stranger were almost impossible. If I had been introduced by someone, then the experience was different. But being in a room with people that I didn't know made me very uncomfortable.

And this shyness followed me into adulthood.

Once I got into the business world, I would put myself behind other leaders and support them in their visions instead of leading my own vision. I have started five businesses in my life, and I've never been the face of those companies.

One of those businesses was a high-end car rental agency in Miami. At one point, I attended an event hosted by the Miami Concierge Association with our team. The idea was to network with all of the hotel and luxury condominium concierges from Miami to present our business and generate new clients. One of my partners made a competition to see who could obtain the most business cards at the event.

I was frozen. I could not — and did not know how — to approach people. Being new in Miami, my English was very poor, and I didn't know where to start. My anxious worry creeped in …

How do I approach this person?

What should I say?

What will they think about me?

At this point in my life, this scenario had become my normal. And I was used to navigating this anxiety.

But, Alan later showed me how essential meeting people is — and how to overcome this fear you need to just talk to everyone.

The second time I met Alan, we were having lunch at the Edition Hotel in Miami Beach. After lunch, we went to the restroom. Right away, Alan walked up to someone who had just washed their hands and offered to shake his hand, saying, "Hello, I am Alan Laz."

His directness with a complete stranger amazed me — I could not believe what was happening!

Who meets someone in the bathroom? And even shakes their hand?

I left the bathroom a bit embarrassed. What would this person think of us?

A minute later, Alan was leaving the bathroom with this person — they spoke for another five minutes, exchanged business cards, and said goodbye with a big hug. I was in shock! I had never seen anything like this in my life.

Over the years, I have watched Alan approach strangers hundreds of times — in hotel lobbies, in security lines at airports, on planes, at restaurants, everywhere! Alan never wastes an opportunity to meet someone new. To him, each introduction could lead to a life-changing, meaningful connection.

Meeting Alan was a game-changer in helping me overcome my shyness. He made it look easy! He has always advised me to tell the world what I am seeking and what I am dreaming. You never know who you are talking with. Maybe that person aligns with your goals.

Once I followed his method, I realized that meeting people isn't so difficult after all.

During a business trip a few years ago, I sat beside a man on my flight and decided to introduce myself. Before meeting Alan, I probably would've kept to myself and avoid conversation. This time, however, I challenged myself. I decided to say hi. I quickly learned that he was a professor at a university in the US who taught public speaking. And his dream was to start his own business as a public speaking coach. Being passionate about entrepreneurship, I encouraged him to follow his heart.

Public speaking is something that I've had to grow my confidence in — my shyness and introverted nature often made public speaking a challenge. So, the fact I met someone whose passion and business focus is public speaking instantly piqued my interest.

We ended up exchanging contact information and have since kept in touch.

And you know what? After our meeting, he did start his company. And I assume he's now happy fulfilling his dream.

Listen, and Make People Feel Seen and Heard

So, what exactly makes it so easy for Alan to meet other people — I'm sure you're wondering, *What in the world does Alan say?*

Well, it's effortless and uncomplicated. Alan simply starts with, "Hello, I am Alan Laz." The other person introduces themself. Next, Alan asks them a personal question.

And the conversation takes off.

Plus, Alan always makes sure to ask everyone their name. And he'll ask people to spell it if necessary.

By doing so, right away, Alan makes everyone feel individually seen and heard. He also reconfirms their name a few minutes later to make sure he remembers well and to reaffirm his interest in each individual.

Time and again in business meetings, I have seen his approach with waitstaff at restaurants. It's astonishing how the simple act of showing the person in front of you that you have interest in knowing and understanding their name — the most introductory and an essential part of their identity — creates a bond. Demonstrating a true interest in people has led to us both being treated like kings at restaurants. In business meetings, before even talking about business, the other party has been willing to do a deal with Alan merely because he extended basic attention, respect, and interest.

If you sit with Alan for two hours, you'll likely talk

for an hour and a half. Alan will begin by sincerely telling you how happy he is to have the opportunity to be meeting you. Secondly, he will briefly introduce himself and his company, and next he will tell you his unbelievable family story. After Alan introduces himself, he will ask about you and will transition to a state of active listening. He will ask questions, one after the other, letting you talk while his mind is analyzing all you tell him.

Later, Alan will often offer advice or make a business proposal.

And over and over, his equation works. Because, people love to be heard.

In fact, when people engage in high-quality listening at work, many operational benefits emerge like superior job performance, better leadership, improved trust — and even lower rates of worker burn-out.[6] Listening also helps people feel understood by others, and this feeling alone can make people happier and healthier.[7] They feel good when someone listens to them and shows interest, especially when someone is asking questions to get to know them more intimately.

Alan has shown me a true leader is one who listens to others more than he or she speaks about themself. Listen to what people have to say and you will constantly be shown how many rewarding opportunities you can find in life.

At **CURATED**, active listening has become part of our company culture. We make a point to be present for people. We ask if they're doing well. We also include their opinions into our decision-making processes.

Recently, we had an employee whom we highly valued who started to lead with negativity. This behavior began to create a heavy atmosphere for people and was affecting morale. Other employees were becoming unhappy and no longer wanting to work with him.

So, we had a decision to make: We could either choose to part ways to avoid furthering a toxic work environment and risk losing other employees. Or, we could listen to him and give him an opportunity to overcome whatever he was going through.

We chose to listen.

First, we offered him a month's paid leave where all he had to do was focus on himself. We even set him up with life coaching support. And then we waited.

After the month was up, we each agreed to have a meeting to learn how the month went, how he was feeling, and if he wanted to return to CURATED. Again, we valued this employee greatly. Ultimately, all that we wanted was his happiness as a person, even if that meant he was ready to move on from our company.

Once we met with him, we asked how he was and how his break went. And he shared all that he was feeling. And he voiced how he realized that he no longer wanted to be in a management position. He also wanted to stay with our company. So, we took to heart how he was feeling. By the end of the meeting, we created a new role for him where he could apply his talents and passions in a way that inspires him — and in a way that also could further help our operations.

So, benefits emerged for both of us.

Had we chosen not to listen, we never would

have learned what was driving his unhappiness. We couldn't have identified how we as leaders and as friends could help him boost his wellbeing, and in turn, improve the business environment for everyone.

By choosing to talk to people and to listen in return, you can foster openness and deepen relationships in ways you may not even have predicted. You can generate opportunities — and even inspire others.

And these connections are what doing business is all about!

HYPNOSIS MEDITATION 

Believe, Behave, Become!

Scan this QR code for a guided hypnosis meditation. This meditation will help you connect your brain with your heart, allowing you to fully experience this chapter's emotions. By doing so, you can embrace its concepts and transform your behavior to align with the person you aspire to become!

JOURNALING

Describe how you talk to others and how you listen. How can you deepen these skills?

**Do you approach strangers
for conversation?**

**What positive outcomes could
happen if you did?**

3

GIVE UNCONDITIONALLY

"Help people from your heart! When you give unconditionally, you receive ten times back."

I have always loved helping people. People often come to me for business or personal advice, and I feel honored to offer perspectives that can help them. I tremendously enjoy supporting them and giving advice.

This interest to help was instilled in my upbringing. As a child, I was raised in a very generous environment. My dad, my mom, and my grandparents always supported everyone that was in need. As a result, giving back and helping people has been a big part of my life's purpose.

However, until recently, I didn't realize that I was focusing my attention of helping others on the wrong priorities — until I learned the hard way.

One week (and early in my time with CURATED), it was my turn to ask for help. I turned to two different friends whom I'd been supporting through something, assuming they'd be willing to help me in return. But instead of reciprocating during my time of need, they each completely ghosted me. Twice in one week!

I was furious and upset.

I wanted validation that I was treated unfairly. So, I turned to my wife (my then-girlfriend). I began complaining that their actions weren't fair because I had always been there for them! I had invested a lot of time and effort supporting them personally and their businesses. But, instead of commiserating with me, she replied, "That is your problem, Jordi. You love supporting people, but you expect something in exchange. This is what makes you so upset about the situation."

Those words shocked me. She was 100% right.

Rather than helping my friends unconditionally, I was expecting something in return. By helping them, I expected them to help me. But this thinking was all backwards — and kept me as a giver focused on myself. And from this mindset, I wasn't truly helping.

I could not stop thinking about this ah-ha moment for days. I realized that so many times in my life I'd helped someone expecting something in return.

And the more I learned about Alan, the more this perspective showed itself.

Help From Your Heart

"When you have the opportunity to help someone, you do it!"

I used to frequently call Alan to thank him for his mentorship and partnership.

"Stop thanking me," he used to say, "I'm the one that should call you to thank you. You gave me an opportunity to help you, and you don't realize how good that feels."

At first, I didn't understand what he was talking about. Why would he thank me for helping me?

Because previously in my life I'd been helping people expecting something in exchange, I wasn't feeling thankful during these exchanges. Instead, I often felt frustrated when people didn't meet my expectation of reciprocity. But, the more I thought about Alan's words and analyzed his actions with others, I started to understand what he was saying.

Genuinely helping others means helping from the heart with no strings attached. And when life gives you opportunities to help, you embrace this moment.

A perfect example of this mindset came one time after meeting with Alan at the LAZ Parking headquarters in Hartford, CT. Alan arranged for one of his drivers to take me to the airport. When I was getting in the car, the driver asked me if I was a LAZ employee or a client, I answered that I was business partners with Alan. His face immediately changed, he went red. I asked if he knew Alan, and his voice changed and softened. He said, "The world needs more people like him."

I agreed with him.

Then he said, nearly in tears, "Alan did something

very special for me that I will never forget. I will always be available for him and his family."

He told me how one day while he was driving Alan, his wife called. They were supposed to take their kids to Disney, but unfortunately, they had recently encountered some unexpected expenses. They no longer could take their vacation. What the driver didn't realize was Alan had heard him say that they would need to cancel the trip. Once they arrived at the airport, as the driver opened the door for Alan, Alan handed him a $5,000 check. He said, "Please take your wife and kids to Disney."

When I heard this story, I was shocked. Alan's generosity changed this family's life. Of course, not all help has to be monetary. But for this driver and his family, the check meant that his kids could take an amazing, memorable trip.

That story inspired me to help others more. And to truly help, I had to do so unconditionally and from the bottom of my heart.

When Alan helps people, he doesn't expect anything in exchange. He always says that when you give unconditionally, you end up receiving 10 times more than you gave. He believes that this is one of the major keys to his life's success.

And we've since embraced this mindset at CURATED.

We encourage everyone to help each other and be available to one another. If you were to ask all our CURATED employees to define our company in one word, 80% of them would say, FAMILY.

And "family" is what a company should be.

We support our employees professionally — and personally. Whenever someone has a financial issue, we are there to give a hand. If someone has a personal issue, the company is there to support — but not only the company, the whole team. Once, one of our employees was navigating a divorce and had to go to court to fight for custody of his daughter. The court was in Texas and the company paid for his flights and hotels. He didn't have any family available to help him through this process. So, I personally went to court with him to support him.

We felt better knowing that our employee wasn't

alone during such a difficult experience.

At the end of the day, this is what a family member is supposed to do. As Alan says, an opportunity to help someone is a gift!

Since I've known Alan, he has had two heart attacks. After the second, I asked him why he wasn't slowing down. I see Alan as someone who has succeeded in life and could start slowing down to enjoy some personal and vacation time. His answer has always been the same, "Jordi, I love to create opportunities for people. I have the privilege to have been able to give work to 15,000 people in my company. I want to continue creating more opportunities."

Alan believes that the best way to help someone is giving them a way to generate income through a job. Or, by helping someone start a business that will grow and generate more opportunities for other people.

A perfect example of this belief lies in a story with a man named John.

A handful of years ago, I was visiting NY with my wife, and Alan found out I was there. Immediately, he sent me a chauffeur to pick me up and drive me to Hartford. I thought the driver was Alan's personal chauffeur, but when I started talking to him, I realized their relationship was so much more. One day, Alan requested a chauffeur service, and this driver, John, was dispatched to drive Alan. While they were in the car, Alan started talking to him and asked him about his life, if he liked his job, and what was his goal. John told Alan that he was saving money to start his own chauffeur company one day. Alan told John, "Come to my headquarters next week with a Business Plan." John didn't even know what a business plan was or how to make one. But, John showed up. And after their meeting, they both started a chauffeur company where the first big client was LAZ Parking.

Today, John owns a successful limousine company called Perfect Rides. And he has created many job opportunities for his employees.

Had Alan not initiated conversation with John and been genuinely interested in him as a person, John probably would never have shared his dream. Perhaps, it would have taken him years longer to start his business. Or perhaps, he never would have started it.

But, Alan chose to open up conversation and listen that day. And by listening, he found an opportunity to help.

When you create an opportunity for someone, you are telling them, "I believe in you." When you feel that someone you respect believes in you, you are going to do everything possible to not fail this person. You are not only doing this for you, but also for the person who afforded you the opportunity and believed in you.

In fact, studies show that stating this belief to people works for boosting performance. When people received performance feedback from leadership with this statement, "I'm giving you these comments because I have very high expectations, and I know that you can reach them," the feedback was 40% more effective in changing people's behaviors.[8] The leader's belief in them was a motivating force.

In thinking back when John and I were buying our first car to sell, a big reason I felt any confidence in being able to raise $750,000 in a matter of days was because Alan said, "I believe in you." At the time, I wasn't confident this capital raise was possible. But, here was someone who hardly knew me, who believed in me more than myself, and wrote a $50,000 check to make it happen! I knew I could not fail this person.

For my business partner and me, that big car deal was the real start of CURATED. After that deal, Alan transitioned from our mentor to our business partner and was instrumental in helping us build a real business.

His belief in creating this opportunity for us changed our lives forever.

When Unexpected Opportunity Gives You Your Life Back

"Before CURATED, I never had the feeling of waking every morning and loving to come to work. It's a beautiful feeling. My happiness has gone all the way up!"

– Reuben

A key employee at CURATED is Ruben. In his 50s, he's an immigrant to the US from the Dominican Republic and one of the most positive and best employees we have.

Before Ruben worked at CURATED, he worked three jobs to get by: at a condominium, a parking valet, and his own car wash service during weekends. For as long as he could remember, he was working 7 days a week, 7 am to 11 pm. And in 20 years, he had never had a vacation. Ruben also barely got to see his family on that schedule, which as a father and a grandfather hurt him greatly.

John first met Ruben when he was a valet at the building that John lived in. He was also washing cars, including John's. Every night and morning, Ruben would cheerfully greet John as he went to get his car. John had never seen anyone so consistently happy. Anytime John arrived home after a hard day, Ruben always cheered him up with the biggest smile, "Hello, Mr. John!" One day, John realized that Ruben was working seven days a week and wondered how he could be so happy working so much. John asked Ruben, "How can I help you? You always help me! We need to find you a better job, Ruben!"

John and I knew that we had to do more for Ruben. Here was this man who's worked his whole life so hard and yet he still needed three jobs to survive. So, we decided to create an opportunity for him: We wanted to hire him to work for us at CURATED. And we'd pay him a salary that enabled him to work one job rather than three. Plus, we'd give him weekends off and vacation time.

The day we met Ruben to offer him a job, he cried. Our offer was unexpected. And he said the tears just fell from happiness that we wanted to help an older man. He hadn't even had any day off in over 20 years!

To us, the opportunity we created for him was fulfilling.

For Ruben, it changed his life.

Giving Second Chances

> *"In my company, it's almost impossible to get fired. You need to really screw up to get fired."*

Alan is a huge believer in second chances (and third, fourth …). The only thing that Alan requests is that the person receiving this second chance is remorseful and willing to improve. He believes in people's ability to change, but only if they really acknowledge that they did something wrong. Without an apology and willingness to change, it doesn't make sense to give a second chance to someone.

Alan believes that you have many ways to help people. He has chosen to elevate humanity through business. Business gives people money, and money gives people security — food, clothes, and a place to live. Money also gives people a way to help other people.

A big example of Alan's second-chance belief is his major endeavor to create 1,000,000 Jobs for people upon their release from prison. LAZ does this effort through the NAACP's Million Jobs campaign, of which Alan sits on the national board. His first effort to this goal is in Connecticut with the aim to create 10,000 new jobs within five years. To date, LAZ has created over 1,000 jobs nationwide for returning citizens at its own company. Alan created this initiative because he learned that 60% of the people released from jail without a job return to prison. Meanwhile, only 15% of people released from jail with a job secured will return. So, his company became part of a program where inmates with life sentences mentor incoming inmates. In jail, these people will train as car detailers. Alan has created a detailing company that operates out of his parking garages. Once the program graduates get out of jail, he hires them at this company. His aim is that they will be able to find a home and will start giving back to the community at least 10 times more than they received.

Alan's goal is to get 1,000 companies involved in the project.

The person leading this project inside LAZ Parking with Alan is an ex-drug dealer that Alan gave an opportunity to as a maintenance worker back in 2004. The man started learning and growing within the company, and today, he is one of the managers and also a pastor in his community.

And this all started because Alan gave someone a chance. And he chose to act consciously in his decision.

From this mindset, conscious businesses have the potential to make a huge impact on our communities. According to Conscious Capitalism®, a conscious business is a company that serves as a value-creating tool to "solve systemic problems, uplift communities, and create meaningful change." Conscious capitalism is a free-market, ethical business model that prioritizes value for all stakeholders: employees, suppliers, communities, society, and the environment.[9]

To me, a conscious business is also one that leads from the heart and prioritizes your humanity by serving with unconditional love. When you lead from this perspective, you create opportunities for communities by:

- Supporting equity
- Investing in others' wellbeing
- Promoting collaboration
- Listening to and acting on others' needs
- Fostering inclusion

Remember in the last chapter when I shared the story about one of CURATED's managers who was creating a toxic environment?

Well, when we chose to give him a month's pay while taking time off for himself, we were choosing to give him more chances. When he came back and shared the changes he was looking for in his work, and we listened and created a new role for him, we were choosing again to give him a chance.

Rather than put our energy in his failure, we put

our belief in his potential. And we allowed him the space to make a decision for what he needed to be happy, whether at CURATED or in his personal life.

And now, this happiness has the ability to impact every other person that he interacts with every day.

Remembering to Set Boundaries

While giving unconditionally, an important lesson I've learned along the way is remembering to also set boundaries.

Remember how Alan will give people second chances — but only to people who apologize and are willing to change? That is a boundary Alan has set in order to be able to give to them unconditionally. They must possess self-awareness and responsibility for their actions.

Ultimately, setting boundaries is about setting expectations. And you foster respect for yourself and for the other person.

Helping other people in life — and in business — is hugely important. However, if you're constantly helping someone without any expectation for them to fulfill their own goals, then you end up enabling repeat behaviors. You can foster their dependency on you. People can take advantage of you. And you can deplete yourself, emotionally, physically, and spiritually.

When we gave a month's paid-leave to our employee as he worked out what was going on and what he wanted in life to be happy, we set a boundary: This was our last attempt at helping him. If this effort didn't produce the behavior change he and we both needed for a healthy workplace, then we each needed to move on. While we would've been very sad to no longer have this employee, we knew that we had to draw a line in how far we'd invest into his wellbeing, personally and professionally, if he was unwilling to act. If we kept helping him and saw no positive change in the workplace, then we would be doing more harm than good for everyone: for him, for the employees he managed, and for our company's morale.

And he respected that we had to draw this line. Further, it showed that we believed in his ability to make decisions about what he needed in his life. Fortunately, his situation ended positively, and we were able to turn a negative moment around into a positive one, for him and for our company.

And that's what setting boundaries can do for you. People know where you stand. And they further understand how they can align their actions with those boundaries — and meet and exceed your expectations.

Doing business from a place of unconditional love doesn't mean letting people walk over you. It means standing up for what's right, advocating for your employees, prioritizing everyone's wellbeing. By leading with love, you foster positivity across your company's entire ecosystem — and this positivity is contagious.[10]

Business no longer becomes about, *How can I be happy?* Instead, you ask, *How can I make others happy and increase the happiness around us?*

HYPNOSIS MEDITATION

Believe, Behave, Become!

Scan this QR code for a guided hypnosis meditation. This meditation will help you connect your brain with your heart, allowing you to fully experience this chapter's emotions. By doing so, you can embrace its concepts and transform your behavior to align with the person you aspire to become!

JOURNALING

In what ways are you helping others find opportunities?

**How can you expand your ability
to give unconditionally?**

4

MAKE IT ABOUT THE PEOPLE

"You are only as good as
the people that you have
working with you."

Have you ever heard of a colonoscopy room in a company?

When I worked at the global company as the operations manager, that's what we called the room where our boss reprimanded us. Remember, our boss was leading us through fear. If anyone made a mistake, he threatened to fire us. When he walked through the hallways, everyone put their heads down and stopped conversation. Needless to say, the energy in the office was heavy.

So, any time our boss said sternly, "Jordi, follow me!" all my colleagues started cooing, *"Ooooooh colonoscopy."*

In my operations role, he used to make me analyze every little expense. I had to meet with all the vendors (telephone, banks, printing machines, gold suppliers, software developers, etc…) and push them to the last penny. That was the only time you could tell he was happy and was feeling proud of me.

Once, I got into trouble because I found out our gold supplier never charged us for a purchase we had made months before. Immediately, I called the supplier to let them know, and obviously, they were super grateful since they had an accounting mistake and had not realized. We were talking 25,000 Euro — a lot of money. When I proudly told my boss that I found the mistake and called them, he became livid with me. "Why did you call them?!" he yelled. "That's their fucking problem!"

The only response I could give was to lower my head with a defeated "Ok." Deep down inside, I knew he wasn't right. *I guess that's just how the business world is,* I thought.

When I arrived in the United States — and before I started CURATED — I had the opportunity to manage a company, Lou La Vie. This was my first time as a General Manager, and it's when I started acting the way I was taught: Compensated employees the least amount possible. Pushed employees hard to deliver as much as they could. Fire anyone who arrived late more than three days in a row. Fire anyone who made a mistake.

Consequently, employees were scared of me. I thought they just respected me, but they actually just wanted to keep their jobs. In less than two years, 13 employees passed through the company. The worst part is that I was proud of this turnover! I never questioned if I was the one that had the problem or if I was causing it. Some of them definitely needed to go, but obviously not 13!

When we started CURATED, this leadership style carried over at first. Even my business partner, John, was scared of me. He used to tell me, "You are too tough on people, bro. You need to relax."

In reality, I was young, scared, and felt I had a lot to prove to myself, my parents, and my friends back in Spain. I wanted to demonstrate that I was capable of succeeding, and this was the way I learned to lead.

Alan opened my eyes. To him, "it's all about the people."

The first thing that I noticed about Alan was he was never upset. I could not believe that someone like him could be so successful in life yet not tough on people. Instead of leading with fear, he was always trying to understand his employees' actions. He puts himself in their shoes. And the most important thing? He forgives employees when they make a mistake!

One of the key success factors for Alan is his People Over Profits approach.

He believes that the most important asset a company can possess is its team. As a result, you must invest in your employees. Give them the chance to grow within the company, to grow in their positions, and to increase their salaries overtime. To do all of that, you need not only to expect them to grow by themselves but to support their growth.

An entrepreneur or a business leader must be a mentor and a teacher. They need to instill the company's values, and at the same time, you have to be open to the concept of listening more than talking.

A lot of entrepreneurs and business leaders exist that talk to their employees. But, they never listen to them. As a leader, you must listen to your employees' professional challenges — as well as their personal obstacles — and to help them when you can. An employee that believes the company listens and helps them will be loyal and will give their best in return.

In fact, employees with very high levels of belonging and engagement are much more likely to feel heard in the workplace.[11] And companies with the most effective listening programs are also four times more likely to keep their employees (even during high attrition) and six times as likely to meet or exceed financial goals.[12]

So, actively engaging with your employees has real benefits to people and to business.

Make Happiness a Priority

> *"You are only as good as the people you have working with you."*

As an employee, I often hated going to work, even when I loved my job. The week that I needed to do something I hated, I was miserable. As a result, I didn't do the task to the best of my ability. And this affected my productivity and happiness in my role.

Sometimes, a job position includes many different roles, and some of them employees may hate doing. But, we are all different.

We like different things, and we are good at different skills and tasks. So, one way of ensuring you optimize how everyone works is to have employees working on the tasks they enjoy. You need to find what people are good at and discuss it with them. Then, if possible, help them obtain an opportunity that fulfills that ability. There's nothing more important in life than doing something you love. Your responsibility as an entrepreneur is to make sure that you help your employees find what they love and support them in this journey. Doing so keeps people happy and motivated.

You may be asking, *Why does this matter? Aren't employees supposed to just do the tasks you tell them, whether or not they like it?*

The reality is not that simple.

Believe it or not, 70% of employees find their sense of purpose in life through their work.[13] Think about that! The majority of people's sense of identity and wellbeing relies on how happy they are in your workplace. Yet, 80% of people go to their job just for a paycheck.[14] That means that most employees experience work as merely a transaction rather than supporting their goal of helping to fulfill their life's purpose.

So, how engaged and fulfilled they are by their responsibilities matters.

When employees view a task negatively, that mindset alone already makes accomplishing the task more difficult for them. They're also more challenged to overcome any obstacles they might need to address along the way. On the flip side, employees who love a task are energized to complete it. When they think of the task from a positive mindset, they can concentrate better, become fully absorbed, and will be more productive. These outcomes lead to more success for them at work.[15]

And remember, companies with more engaged employees are more successful at exceeding their financial goals.

Today at CURATED, I ensure that an employee only does what they love to do 80 to 90% of the time. This way, they're inspired to work and feel fulfilled with their responsibilities. I'd rather hire someone else to do the tasks they dislike, someone with the specific experience and loves it. The energy of a company where everyone does what they love doing is indescribable.

You create an unstoppable company, full of joy.

To do so, you also have to address happiness holistically. Rather than solely focus on the roles they serve, you should also address their happiness as a person.

I once read a quote from the General Manager of LAZ Parking in Florida that said, "Success can be measured by happiness from the people that surround you and the fulfillment of your goals." LAZ Parking currently has two life coaches available to all the employees, as well as their own leadership training program to support employees and help them grow. In fact, they have their own LAZ university in the workplace that focuses on fostering employee wellness and skills development.

After seeing the LAZ model of prioritizing happiness and its success, we've since implemented this focus at CURATED. Today, employee wellness is at the forefront of how we support them.

Each Monday, we do a 30-minute group coaching session with our employees. This gives them the opportunity to open up about successes they've had, actions employees did they appreciated — essentially, they have space to have a voice. And we start the week with positive energy. Some sessions our employees lead; these are required attendance. During them, we'll discuss:

1. Personal and professional wins — what great things have happened to them the previous week.
2. The company values — who's been embracing them this week. We give positive "shout outs" to these employees.
3. Gratefulness exercise — where we share an employee we're grateful for and why.
4. An employee life story — a personal experience that someone is going through. This allows us all to be more empathetic with one another by better understanding our lives.
5. A group meditation.

The energy after these meetings is amazing! Everyone feels so enthusiastic about the week and connected as people and friends.

Other sessions, our life coach leads. We offer this life coaching to all our employees. And they can choose whether they want to attend these sessions. So far, only one employee has opted out. We have themes built out for each quarter's session:

Q1: Physical (sleep, exercise, nutrition, vitamin D)

Q2: Emotions

Q3: Self-limiting beliefs

Q4: Addictions (and similar topics)

We also host three offsite retreats each year — open to any employee who wants to come. The goal is to help people get outside of their workplace responsibilities and develop as a person. We offer sessions in breathwork and meditation, and other wellness-minded activities.

Since prioritizing happiness, we've seen morale improve and a boost in productivity.

Happy and motivated employees are better at their jobs. And this positive force also supports better results for the company, and at the end of the day, more money and opportunities for everyone — new and old employees. As the workplace trends to hiring younger employees, specifically Generation Z, employee happiness must be on your radar. Gen Z greatly prioritizes their mental health wellness — and they are especially purpose driven.[16]

A happy employee that feels supported and believes in the company's values will share them with the clients, vendors, friends, and family. By doing so, they help to improve the overall communities they live in. This ripple effect pays forward the positivity.

So invest in them, and make sure they're successful and happy in all parts of their lives.

Inspire Ownership in Employees

Another happiness tenet I learned from Alan is to make sure that each employee acts as though the company is theirs. You want to ensure that the people who help grow the company not only make a salary — but also participate in the value they helped create over the years.

One way you can inspire ownership is through how you choose to compensate employees.

One of Alan's most awe-inspiring stories revolves around a day when he sold a substantial stake in LAZ Parking for a staggering amount of money. Now, the LAZ management team is scattered across the country. To share the exciting news and express his gratitude to the entire management team, Alan and his partners called 58 people who'd earned equity in LAZ over the years. They awarded those loyal employees with a total of $35 million! Some of those employees started as parking attendants.

Think about the impact this decision made on people's lives!

Alan and his team could've chosen to keep those profits themselves. Or even invest that money in a different manner. Instead, they chose to invest it into their people, further fueling their People Over Profits philosophy.

As a result, employees received a substantial amount of money that could greatly affect their financial future — while feeling respected and valued for their contributions. The company's success was their success, too!

At CURATED, we've followed suit.

In 2020 — after we'd been partnering with Alan for five years — we sold 25% of CURATED to the former CEO of Sequoia Capital (and number 1 tech investor in the world for 5 years), Jim Goetz. The day we signed the contract and the money hit our accounts was unlike anything I'd experienced. I'd always dreamed of this moment and thought that I would feel the most incredible emotion to see that amount of money. I mean, obviously, I felt proud that we had accomplished something — and felt good that my soon-to-be-born baby would have financial stability — but some feeling was missing. I didn't feel the ecstasy I anticipated I would.

That feeling would soon change.

The following day, the first thing we did was to share part of this profit with our employees. Without them, we would have never achieved this dream.

So, we had each person join us individually in the conference room to tell them, "Thank you." We also shared that they would receive a check the size of which we based on the years they'd worked in the company — and not the job position within the company. Seeing their faces, their eyes, and their reactions was the best feeling I had in my life.

They were shocked!

For some of them, the amount of money was huge and was a big part of their annual salary. Surprised by this action, some people didn't know what to say, some were laughing, some cried. John and I had to make a massive effort to hold our tears, and when everyone left the room, we looked at each other and said, "We are definitely doing something right here." Then, we both cried.

At that moment, everything I had been learning from Alan the previous five years of my life started making sense. The puzzle I'd been putting together from his mentorship and partnership so far suddenly started connecting to reveal a beautiful picture.

Inspiring Your Employee's Dreams

Marquise was the car detailer for CURATED who had been working with us since before founding our company at our luxury car rental company, Lou La Vie. He had a troubled past in his personal life from some decisions he made and had gotten into jail a couple of times. But we wanted to give him an opportunity and genuinely appreciated him as a person.

So, he became a dedicated employee of CURATED.

What we didn't know was that Marquise always dreamed of becoming a truck driver. However, he didn't have enough money to pursue this career. So, he kept this part of himself tucked away.

The day we decided to share the profit of selling ownership in our company, little did we know this action helped change his life. Some days after Marquise received his share of profit, he came to John and me to let us know about his dream to be a truck driver. And now that he had this extra money in his life, pursuing this passion was now possible. He could now realize his dream.

So, Marquise ended up leaving CURATED, but he made his dream true! He got his truck driver license and started driving a truck, and began making a lot more money to support his family.

While we lost a valuable employee, we gained fuller hearts knowing he was fulfilling his life's dream.

When you do things from your heart and are helping people, that's when you've unlocked the real secret of happiness.

I'd always thought happiness would come from something material. But that day — and since prioritizing our employees' happiness — I've realized that the more you give and the more opportunities you create for people, the happier you are.

And happiness beats a colonoscopy room any day.

HYPNOSIS MEDITATION

Believe, Behave, Become!

Scan this QR code for a guided hypnosis meditation. This meditation will help you connect your brain with your heart, allowing you to fully experience this chapter's emotions. By doing so, you can embrace its concepts and transform your behavior to align with the person you aspire to become!

JOURNALING

How do you currently prioritize employee happiness?

**What can you do to deepen this
for them?**

5

ENHANCE THE POSITIVE THINGS ABOUT PEOPLE

"Motivate people, and let them know what you see in them — You are the best!"

When I was working for other people, I always assumed that my bosses valued me, despite them not telling me so.

I knew I was a hard worker and overdelivering on what I was asked to do. I also had an entrepreneur mindset and was always bringing new things to the table to improve the company.

But, the only way I knew they believed I was doing a good job was when they would give me more projects and promotions. At 24 years old, I was in meetings with all the big managers — this was how they showed they counted on me. But, no one ever told me. No one ever called me to a meeting to thank me for what I was doing.

The only time all of them talked to me about the future was the day that I told them I was leaving the company. That day, they expressed all those great plans they had but never before shared with me.

What a shame to never voice appreciation until the day someone leaves. And what a missed opportunity to foster greatness within your company and for your employees.

When employees receive regular recognition, an array of benefits emerge: Morale improves. Performance strengthens. Employee retention increases. And productivity soars. Even customer satisfaction greatly benefits. And these trends hold true no matter the industry you work in.[17]

When you offer people recognition, you also have the opportunity to give them a positive boost in their day. You don't always know what people are going through. Some employees may be coming to work depressed or upset about something. They may feel challenged or defeated with something they're hoping for. Or maybe they have a sick family member at home.

Point is, we bring a world of emotions and aspects of ourselves with us to work every day, whether others realize it or not. And, it actually can take very little effort to make people feel recognized.

For example, every time Alan calls me, one of the first things he says is, "You are the best!"

No matter how many times I hear this sentiment, I instantly smile and it makes my day. And Alan applies this behavior outside of the workplace, too.

Once, I was in the car driving Alan to the airport. He was flying to Las Vegas for a parking convention and wanted to make sure his reservation was correct. So, he called the receptionist. When talking to her, Alan was speaking with the most wonderful words and being extra nice. When he hung up, I asked him why he did that. I thought maybe that woman would think he was making fun of her by being so nice.

He looked at me shocked about my question. "Are you serious, Jordi? What does it take to make somebody's day? Today, she will go home with a smile on her face."

And he does exactly the same thing with valet parkers, waitresses at restaurants, employees, everyone! He always makes sure that he makes someone's day!

Since realizing this perspective, I now make a point to do the same with our employees at CURATED.

One thing I'll do is to walk our showroom and the mechanic shop with the goal to talk to every single person and see first-hand the wonderful things they're doing. Since I hear about these efforts in our Monday meetings, I like seeing for myself our employees while they're hard at work. I'll use my lunch time to connect with each person and say things like, "I hear you're doing a great job! Thank you!" By doing so, I show each person that I see them, I value them, and I'm here for them. You can tell how much they appreciate this recognition! Their faces instantly light up!

Another time, after I came back from a business trip, one of the first people I saw in the office was one of our employees, who is always so happy and just a great person. When I saw him, I was genuinely excited to see him. So, I told him and gave him a big hug. The next day, I received a text message from this employee that he wanted to see me. In the past, we've helped him with some financial assistance when he needed it. So, I thought he may be reaching out to me for this reason. But once we talked, I was completely wrong. He told me how when I saw him yesterday and hugged him, he was so amazed. He went home that day to tell his wife what happened and that he felt so wonderful knowing that I missed him and was excited to see him.

He wanted me to know how much my gesture meant to him!

From my perspective, I was just greeting a friend hello. From his perspective, I was making him feel important and loved. And how beautiful is that!

Everyone Is a Good Person

"Find the good in people."

When I started spending time with Alan, one of the things that shocked me the most was his trust in people from the onset.

Once, Alan and I were involved in a business deal. We were in a meeting with the other party, and I had a bad feeling about them. He's such a nice person that I worried they were trying to take advantage of him. So, I told him, "Alan, they aren't good people."

In response, he said, "Jordi, that's the difference between you and me. I believe that everybody is a good person."

That sentence touched me profoundly.

Before meeting Alan, I didn't fully trust people. I believed that everyone wanted to take advantage of everyone else. So, you had to be always careful and watch your back. I used to say, "People don't change."

I believed that you should just forget about making a difference in people, because they are who they are — you can't change anyone. And, I certainly didn't think that everyone was a good person. The concept of "unconditionality" didn't even exist in my mind. To do something for someone without expecting anything in exchange was foreign to me. If you did something for someone, then you were expecting this person to help you down the road when you needed it.

So, when Alan called me out on this mindset, it forced me to confront my own limitations. I evaluated how I was thinking about people and the prejudices that lived in my mind, which was absolutely affecting how I assessed situations every day in my life, professionally and personally.

That same day, Alan told me about someone I was dealing with who had disappointed me, "Don't get defensive. Forgive them; they made a mistake. Teach them. Change them."

I spent months thinking about this advice. Remember, I had learned to fire people for mistakes. So, teaching someone and forgiving them shook my foundation of what it meant to be a leader.

Of course, my experiences with Alan have destroyed this mindset, as well as the personal growth I've gained from working with two coaches. Since meeting them, I myself am a completely different person than I used to be. I've always been me, but I've grown and evolved — and changed. And for the better. I also now believe that everyone is a good person; those who "aren't good" have past experiences, emotions, and behaviors that they must heal.

Over time, I've been able to properly appreciate and intuit what Alan meant and how to apply this perspective in real life. When someone acts in a way that we don't view as correct, we often become defensive and come from a place of harshness. But by reacting defensively, we close ourselves off and limit the possibility of reaching an agreement and unfolding opportunity. As Alan says, we need to believe that everyone has good intentions. We need to reframe our reaction to accept that the deed we believe to be incorrect was not done to hurt us. Instead, view the situation that the person made a mistake. Now, you have the opportunity to forgive them and show them a better way to help them. To do so, you must lead with love for the other person.

And admittedly, this teaching has been one of the most difficult lessons for me to apply. I've had to unwind years of behavior and rewire my basic response mechanisms.

Today, I regard this approach as a key principle to the way I operate in business and in life. Still, it requires effort. That said, the results are incredible! When people see your nice, fair, and friendly reaction to their "not that friendly" actions, they're shocked. This unexpected reaction is confusing and disarming — and transforms an adversary from a foe to a friend.

I have seen this effect everywhere: with employees, vendors, clients. Because the traditional business world doesn't typically operate on this model, new employees often aren't accustomed to such kindness. So, when they see people treating them and others so well, they become shocked and in disbelief, and sometimes, they put boundaries up and rudeness sets in. They believe there's some other intention beyond this caring response.

But as soon as they realize that our unconditionality is real and genuine, they quickly relax and embrace it.

And this response can be the same with new clients and vendors.

The car industry can be tough, and unfortunately, not the most respected. So, clients have gotten used to being taken advantage of in their other business relationships. And they'll often approach our new relationship cautiously. Often, they're shocked at how nice everyone at our company is — and sometimes become suspicious that it's just so that we make a lot of money from them. Over time, however, they realize that we truly care about their happiness.

And we develop long-term relationships built on trust and respect as a result.

Mentorship — Help Them Grow

"I believe that in business, everybody needs mentors, because we all have ups and downs in life. When you can get a helping hand or be inspired by

somebody, it's a gift."

When I was studying in Spain, I read about the figure of "the mentor." I always thought that was a cool idea, but it was unrealistic in Spain.

At one point, I worked for a company where my main clients were across Europe in Spain, Portugal, France, and Italy. At some point, I asked my boss if the company would pay 50% of a French course so that I could perform better at work. I offered to pay for half of the course and to study after work hours. My boss refused, no further discussion.

I couldn't believe it!

Why would he not help invest in my skills to better serve him and his business? I was not asking for them to pay for an MBA. I was only asking for a French course to be able to do my job better. Their refusal sent a signal to me that I was not worth even that much of an investment into my growth as a person and a professional.

So for this reason (and others), I left. If I was going to keep missing opportunities in my life, then

I had no reason to stay.

Once I met Alan, I finally understood exactly what having and being a mentor meant. Sometimes when we are young, we tend to believe we know everything in business. That attitude leads us to make many mistakes, and most importantly, it costs precious time. We'll tend to focus on doing things the wrong way by allowing our ego to dictate our worth and pride. However, leading with ego can be one of the least effective ways to grow as a person and make business decisions — and acting from the heart instead of ego is one of the most successful traits about Alan.

Before John and I call Alan for our planning chats, he asks that we have a list of potential solutions to our problems. His goal is for us to discuss our ideas together. To do this effectively, we have to leave ego at the door and come open to the possibility that we may not know the right answer on our own.

After our conversations with him, we rarely choose a solution that we suggested. Instead, we create a new one from the other ideas we all brought to the table. During this brainstorm, it's amazing to see how an experienced business person sees the world so differently. Alan helps us think about our obstacles and how to see them through his eyes, his years of experience, and even mistakes he's navigated years before. Alan's guidance has helped us accelerate our growth immensely.

And studies show that mentorship really works.

Seventy-five percent of executives say that they credit their success to having mentors.[18] And employees with mentors are twice as likely to be engaged at work — and 98% more likely to strongly agree they'll recommend where they work as a great employer.[19] And many other benefits emerge, like increased salaries, promotions, and retention rates.

At CURATED, we employ about 28 individuals and have half a dozen partners across many different projects. We not only support all our employees but push them to study and grow professionally as much as they can.

With this goal, the best part of my job is managing and mentoring them: Seeing them grow, helping them do their job, and learning from each one of them. They all are 100% better than me in their specific areas of expertise. I genuinely thrive on helping them grow professionally and financially. I spend most of my time with the team making sure they are happy and fulfilled with their job. I always tell them that they must grow professionally as much as possible, and that if they do, their pay rate — whether with us or elsewhere — will increase exponentially.

Because ultimately, your employee's life at your company will probably be a chapter within their careers. When you mentor them and help foster their growth, you help them ensure success in their own lives. You invest your time and expertise into their futures beyond what their value serves in your own company.

Remember how the majority of employees find their sense of purpose in life through their work?

Your mentorship not only is about their success as a professional, you're helping them find their life's purpose and direction. You're fostering their belief in their own value and worth as a person. And you have the opportunity to make a difference in their ultimate life satisfaction.

And that, my dear friends, is one of the most valuable gifts life can offer you.

HYPNOSIS MEDITATION

Believe, Behave, Become!

Scan this QR code for a guided hypnosis meditation. This meditation will help you connect your brain with your heart, allowing you to fully experience this chapter's emotions. By doing so, you can embrace its concepts and transform your behavior to align with the person you aspire to become!

JOURNALING

What do you normally see first in people, the good or the bad? Why?

In what ways do you support your employee's growth as people?

**How can you elevate
these opportunities?**

6

CELEBRATE THE WINS

*"Come on! Let's give
everyone a standing 'O'!"*

Before meeting Alan, I wasn't the most positive person. While I was overall friendly and smiley, I often operated from a place of what wasn't working.

In life and business, I put very little energy — if any — into acknowledging what was working. When we solved problems at work, I didn't even celebrate the solutions. Instead, I felt the drudgery of having to get past the next problem. Consequently, at CURATED and throughout my leadership experiences, I was infusing my companies and employees with this mindset.

And what a drag this was — and I didn't even realize it!

So, the first time I saw the LAZ Parking "Standing O," I was amazed.

Whenever Alan hears of people doing a good job, he stands up and says, "Let's give him or her a standing ovation!" And he encourages everyone around him to do the same, clap their hands, and recognize the job well done. No matter if there's three people in the group or more, Alan stands. I've even seen him do it over the phone.

The energy that a standing ovation generates in a room full of people is invigorating. Having everyone stand up for a group ovation vibrates happiness and empowers the whole room. And the entire group and individual connects even deeper with the project and the people around it.

When we put a lot of effort into something and end up doing a good job, we all like to be recognized. There's nothing more motivating than your boss — or someone that you respect and admire — telling you, "You did an excellent job!" That acknowledgement encourages you to strive to do it even better next time.

Studies back this thinking up.

When looking at what makes employees have a "best" or "worst" day, progress on a project with a group or individually creates the "best days" for employees. And a big catalyst for this feeling is receiving words of respect and encouragement.[20] Days when employees have a worst day correlates to days when they also had the least amount of respect and encouragement. These positives also are good for the company overall. Employees have less conflict, they work more efficiently, and they create even more successes.[21]

In 2024, I went to an annual LAZ employee gathering. One of the most incredible things to witness was the power of the Standing O. Over the course of three days, they had over 200 standing ovations! Think about the power and energy in that room that resulted from 300 people doing standing ovations together constantly. And it wasn't something that was forced — this was their genuine response to recognizing others.

Celebrating each other is simply part of their LAZ DNA. And you could tell everyone felt happier because of it.

Ring the Bell

In 2017, two years after founding CURATED, Alan invited my wife and I to spend a weekend with him and his family in Hartford. On Monday, Alan wanted us to visit the LAZ headquarters. That morning, he said, "Join me — you guys are going to learn something today!"

Little did I know that morning would turn into one of the most impactful business experiences of my life.

Each Monday, LAZ Parking does their weekly WIN call. And I had the opportunity to join that day's meeting. In this call, all of the managers from each state where LAZ Parking has a presence meet once a week to celebrate their wins.

Here's the process: Alan shouts the name of each state and asks for their weekly wins. That state's manager voices their successes. Then, Alan goes to a huge vintage bell in his office and enthusiastically rings it. Delighted, everyone cheers and claps. And they continue this process until they celebrate every single win.

I was floored. And baffled. And energized! I'd never seen anything like this before in business. I had to know more.

That night while having dinner, I asked Alan why he only focused on the wins. Why not also address the issues, since all of the teams were on the call? His reason was to start the week on a positive note and emphasize celebration among the management team. By doing so, he gets everyone pumped up for the week ahead. Afterward, Alan could help his managers resolve issues individually.

I spent months thinking about that perspective. This concept challenged me to the core.

After reflecting on Alan's focus on celebrating the wins, I realized that he was completely right. If they had used that time during the meeting to also review the challenges each state was facing, the energy would've deflated. The call would become longer.

The people become less energized. And nobody would leave excited and ready to start the week.

So, I began to change my mindset.

Today, I believe it's extremely important to put energy into recognizing the wins. When operations work well, that takes a lot of effort from many people! It's important to recognize those efforts.

At CURATED, we have many ways that we acknowledge successes. One opportunity is through weekly meetings.

Each Monday, we gather as a team, and one of the first things we ask people to do is to publicly recognize and thank someone if they saw or experienced something positive the week before. We've had people thank other employees for something as simple as making them coffee. But, the employee who was making Cuban coffees didn't realize the impact he was making on everyone. This small gesture was making everyone so happy! And it was so wonderful to see that employee get recognized for his kindness. Seeing everyone smile and feel genuinely appreciated — sometimes not even realizing that their action positively affected someone — is always invigorating. We also start the week with a deepened connection between employees. The energy is quite magical.

We also recognize people quarterly.

At the end of each quarter, we host a company meeting that we call "The State of the Company." In this meeting, we remind everyone of the company's higher purpose and discuss the meaning of it. Then, each department head presents the wins their department had during that quarter. After going over these successes, we present the Values Awards where we publicly acknowledge people for their efforts and how well they aligned with our company's five core values.[3] And everyone participates in this recognition. A week before the event, we send a survey to all employees that asks them whom we should recognize this quarter, and why? We identify a person for each value. The person with the most submissions wins an award.

This moment is beautiful, because it makes the

---

3   Our company's core values are: 1. Use Your Heart. 2. Play the Part. 3. Be Authentic. 4. Align to the Dream/CURATED. 5. Own It. And our company's higher purpose is: CURATED, Where Dreams Drive and Passion and History are preserved for generations.

award winners realize that their team sees them and recognizes them. Plus, it's a great exercise for the whole team to connect to our greater values, live those values, and see others live them. After having this meeting, we then host quarterly off-site gatherings. These moments focus on camaraderie with events like go-karting, dinner, bowling, and mini golf.

Since recognizing these wins and positive moments, we've seen morale jump. Employees also have become closer from these experiences.

And now, I can't imagine doing business any other way!

HYPNOSIS MEDITATION

Believe, Behave, Become!
Scan this QR code for a guided hypnosis meditation.
This meditation will help you connect your brain
with your heart, allowing you to fully experience this
chapter's emotions. By doing so, you can embrace its
concepts and transform your behavior to align with
the person you aspire to become!

JOURNALING

**How do you currently recognize
employee achievements
and milestones?**

How could you celebrate the wins more profoundly?

7

BRING YOUR HUMANITY TO BUSINESS

"Who are you helping?
There you have
your answer."

Up until knowing Alan, I made all of my business decisions from a place of: *What's best for my company and me?*

I analyzed profit over loss. I poked holes to find inefficiencies. I identified what was the most cost-effective choice and who was offering me more. And all this perspective kept me solely focused inward on the business and its and my success or failure.

Everything changed once I met Alan.

In the beginning of my mentorship with him, I'd been questioning a business decision all day. I had two different options. Both looked good for the company, so I wasn't sure which decision to go with. Then, Alan called. I explained the decision dilemma I was in. And he asked me, "Whom are you helping in each decision?"

I answered, "Well, they both are good for the company."

"Think about the effects of your choice," he said. "If we chose option one, whom would we help? If we chose option two, whom would we help? How will our decision create more opportunities for people, option 1 or 2?"

I was shocked.

I had never thought about making a decision by understanding how this choice could help others.

After our discussion, I couldn't stop thinking about this perspective. Alan had genuinely challenged my way of thinking and what it means to do business. Prioritizing other people's happiness as a way to conduct business requires you to pause and really be mindful. And to get outside of your own ego. Business is about much more than just doing a service or selling a product — ultimately, you're entering relationships with others every day. Businesses are formed by people! From the vendors you work with to the employees you hire to the customers and clients you serve. Every one of those relationships are people connecting with people. And you have an opportunity in each moment to prioritize humanity and lead from this mindset.

So, you must not look only for monetary gain — you also need to look at the impact. With this thinking, some decisions may bring less cash into the business in the short term. In the long term, however, you will create a much bigger impact on the community.

After understanding his question, I had the answer! Option 2 would create a bigger opportunity for one of our vendors, who was a smaller company. This could, in turn, have a bigger impact on their employees, too. Option 1 was a major company where our business would have less impact. Once I framed it from this perspective, the answer was obvious.

So, what does "prioritize humanity" even mean?

Alan is a big believer that capitalism should elevate humanity through business and create a win-win for people.

Notice that I didn't say, a win-win for companies. That angle keeps business focused on the company and transactions. Oftentimes, business people will look at something and think they're addressing a win/lose situation. *If I do this ABC, then this XZY will or will not happen for my company.* In this equation, we don't even consider humanity. We only address 1) our personal actions and 2) our company's success or failure.

To bring your humanity to business, Alan believes you must focus on the people. You must care about their wellbeing. You must also care about their communities (this includes caring about the environment) — and how your actions are positively influencing their lives. Making business decisions from the perspective of how it helps someone else is the ultimate expression of love — because you genuinely consider their happiness and wellbeing. To arrive at a decision, you can't just look at a spreadsheet and crunch numbers. Focusing on humanity and helping others means you have to know that person. And doing so may take more time. You need more awareness of who they are, what situations they're in. This requires more consciousness around the effect of your actions and decisions.

So, you no longer do what's good for business. You do what's good for humanity. And what's good for humanity will be good for business, too.

Prioritize People Over Profits

"When you have the opportunity to help someone, you do it!"

I've heard Alan say this statement so many times — helping others is simply part of his business DNA.

Alan's People Over Profits philosophy is how he and LAZ Parking center their actions on bringing humanity to business. Alan believes that when you genuinely give of yourself and help others, then that decision comes back to you tenfold. And really to him, this focus all boils down to one factor: being a good human being.

When LAZ is hiring people to work with them, they look at the entire person. People join companies in different phases of their lives. Some are immigrants. Some are former prisoners that are returning citizens. Some are new college graduates. Everyone is different. When you hire from a place of humanity and helping others, you focus on giving people the opportunity to grow and succeed. You elevate their roles. And you invest in the whole person, not just what they can do for your company.

Take for example someone who is fresh out of the prison system. By focusing on their humanity — and not judging them solely by their past actions — you have the opportunity to change their life trajectory. Or, take the immigrant who is seeking a better life — you have the opportunity to help them put their lives ahead. Perhaps, these opportunities are ones that were never available to them before. Leading with empathy and care for others can truly make a difference in their lives and their families.

At CURATED, we've completely embraced this

mindset.

Today, when we hire new employees, we focus on the person and the long term. First, we look at what their values are as a person and if those values align with our company. Then, we look at the skills they have, but we don't obsess over this factor. If a person has shared values and a willingness to learn, then they can learn the skills. And, if we have two people who seem similar in what they bring as candidates, we then focus on the long term: *Who can we help the most? Whose life will change more as a result of working with us?* By answering this question, we have our answer.

If employees want an opportunity to deepen a skill, we'll help them pay for it. For example, when one of our employees (who was an emigrant from Latin America) started with CURATED, his English skills weren't very strong. So, we paid for him to have a private English teacher. Today, he's fluent — and this helps not only his work at our company, but his overall life and connection within his community. And we now often support employees in this way if their English skills are limited.

Another time, one of our mechanics who's in his 50s wanted to pursue a certification to become a manager. At his age, he knew that his body wouldn't be able to keep up with the physical demands of the job, so he wanted to find a way to shift into a new role. He approached us to ask for Fridays off so he could go to school for this certification. We not only gave him Fridays off, but we also paid 50% of his course (which was thousands of dollars), so he could attend. And he did — and is super happy in his role, today.

We also stand up for our employees.

If someone is having personal issues, we're there. Once, one of our employees ended up on life support after a hip surgery. The hospital wanted to send him to another facility, not believing he'd recover. This employee didn't have any family to help him. So, we made phone calls to the hospital and finally talked to the CEO and advocated for him and the treatment we believed he needed. And they changed their decision and kept him in their care. As a result, he ended up getting off life support and fully recovered. Had we followed traditional business philosophy and just focused on our company, perhaps we would've never mixed ourselves in with his hospital needs. We would've just waited for our employee to recover (or not).

Another time, one of our employees had a four-year-old son who died. He became depressed, started drinking at night, and was struggling with life. At work, his attitude became very variable. Overall, he didn't know how to manage his emotions. So, we helped him get access to therapy to help him heal and recover. Today, he's not only recovered — he's so committed to personal growth and always ready to try something new to strengthen as a person. He also brings incredible value to our company and the whole team. One of our best decisions was investing in him as a person and supporting his happiness.

Further, Alan believes that as a leader you also have a responsibility to teach your fellow vendors and partners about what bringing humanity to business means. They either are or aren't on board with you. If they are, then you've helped them open up to a new way to do business. If they aren't, then you've just realized that you probably need a new vendor.

Over time, prioritizing people over profits has become my way of making decisions. And the results are incredible.

At CURATED, we support our vendors as much as we do our employees. We consider them part of the family. When someone works with us, we make sure that whatever agreement we have is a win for both parties. There's nothing more important than ensuring that the person working with your company is excited and happy to be performing that service. Further, they need to feel that you're compensating them for what the service is worth.

Many times, vendors have made mistakes with estimates, and we ended up supporting them by paying more. A couple of times, a vendor had a business issue and needed some money to move forward. In these instances, we've supported them, too. I can guarantee you, those vendors have never forgotten the support, and they have become our most loyal vendors.

When we work with clients, we also focus on helping and prioritize people over profits.

One of our rules when we sell a car is that we should be able to buy that car back from a client at the same price if they needed to sell. We never take advantage of a client. We always sell a car for the market or below market price, and we have been lucky enough that our industry has appreciated, so we have been able to purchase many cars back from our clients with a large profit for them. As a result, our client-retention rate is remarkably high.

And seeing the results of leading business from this mindset is amazing.

When we started CURATED, we made the most optimistic business plans. Alan even told John and me that he didn't have confidence in them — the numbers were too high. Over the years, however, we have exceeded those projections by more than 10 times. And we adamantly believe that we never would be where we are today had we not prioritized people over profits.

And studies show that we're not alone in these outcomes.

"Conscious capitalists" companies have shown

10-year investment returns that are 1025% versus 122% for the S&P 500.[22] Think about that — a 903% difference in investment returns! Similarly, purpose-driven companies over a 20-year period had a 13.6% compound annual growth rate, 5 times higher than the S&P 500.

JUMP Associates studied 15 purpose-driven companies and compared them to other leading companies from the same industries. If you had invested $10,000 on each of those 15 companies in 2000 (so a total of $150,000), by 2019 you would have an ending balance of $1,935,719. But, if you had invested that same amount of money in leading comparable companies, you would've only had $693,731. And you would have even less at $475,614 if you'd invested in the S&P 500. The portfolio of 15 purpose-driven public companies achieved a compound annual growth rate of 13.6% over the 20 years, compared to the 5.9% annual return of the S&P 500 index. In other words, purpose-driven firms deliver 5 times the total return of the S&P 500.[23]

You can choose people over profits and still build

an incredibly profitable business.

Why? Because caring for and helping others matters. Prioritizing people's wellbeing matters. Giving opportunities to people matters. Treating others with respect matters.

And when you choose to bring humanity to business, you're deciding that you'll use your business to make a positive impact in people's lives. That you'll lead from a place of unconditional love.

As my partner John says, with this mindset, you're creating something way bigger than a team or a company. You're building respect, friendships — components in life that are irreplaceable. You're setting stones that people will never forget. They'll take these stones with them and go out in their lives, whether at the grocery store or a board meeting, and they'll pay it forward with the same respect and compassion you've shown them.

You generate positivity simply by prioritizing their humanity — and what's more beautiful in life than that?

HYPNOSIS MEDITATION 

Believe, Behave, Become!

Scan this QR code for a guided hypnosis meditation. This meditation will help you connect your brain with your heart, allowing you to fully experience this chapter's emotions. By doing so, you can embrace its concepts and transform your behavior to align with the person you aspire to become!

JOURNALING

How can you reframe your business decisions to focus on prioritizing your humanity?

Identify a business decision you've made that, after reading this chapter, you realize you could have acted differently.

How would you act today?

8

NEGOTIATE FROM THE HEART

"I don't look at losing or winning."

Back in Spain, I studied negotiation to support my business and law degrees. Once I met Alan, he challenged everything I learned!

In school, all negotiation strategies focused inwardly — *what do we want to accomplish on our side of a deal?* This framework left little, if any, room to think about what could benefit the other parties of the negotiation.

Then, once I entered the business world, I was often pushed to negotiate with vendors and banks, learning directly from how my boss negotiated deals.

The goal was to get as much out of them as I could. Every situation was approached as a battle and a conflict. So, I began to believe that negotiation was like a war. You either win or you lose! Every time I met a vendor, I felt strongly — knowing I was going to win that battle — that I was going to make sure they would nearly lose money on my account. The only way to see my boss excited was by going back to him and showing how much he would save thanks to my negotiation.

And this perspective became normal for me. Even books I read on negotiation after college reinforced this belief.

A few years after meeting Alan, we embarked on a new project together. We spent a weekend in Miami with our future partners in a business deal, negotiating how we would structure it in the United States. I attended as a spectator and didn't talk during our meetings. I was simply watching Alan and the two British gentlemen negotiate.

During their meeting, the British guys made Alan an offer, and he told them that the deal wasn't fair.

They were shocked at Alan's reaction — but even more shocked when they realized that Alan meant that they were giving away too much into Alan's benefit. So, Alan counteroffered more equity to them, and they did the same. I felt like I was in a comedy show.

After the meeting was over, I told Alan, "Alan, I think we lost this negotiation. It was clear that we could have gotten way more out of this deal."

Alan looked at me, smiled, and said, "I don't look at losing or winning, Jordi." Then he asked, "Would you rather have 50% of a company that will one day be worth $100M or 80% of a company that will maybe be worth $10- or $20M?"

I was amazed! I'd never looked at a deal this way.

When talking through this perspective, he told me, "If you can't negotiate a deal where there is a real win-win for both parties, then that opportunity isn't worth investing your time. You need to make sure that the other party benefits the same or more than you, so they are motivated to invest money, time, and energy into the project."

At that moment, Alan destroyed all of my negotiation beliefs.

Reflecting further, I realized how right Alan was! Negotiations are all people forming relationships with each other. Everyone has emotions, wants, needs, and desires — everyone also wants to leave the negotiation feeling happy and valued. By prioritizing this happiness for everyone, you encourage trust between one another. You can even foster friendship. Because at the end of the day, no one wants to do business with someone they don't like or that they think is taking advantage of them. And these feelings can lead to even better outcomes.

In fact, research shows that when you lead with anger and competition in negotiation, you worsen the outcome. You have more conflict, decrease joint gains, and encourage retaliation on the other party. You also are less able to identify each other's interests in a deal. This environment all leads to more conflict and more deal's not closing.[24]

Cooperation and collaboration, however, do the

exact opposite. Ultimately, the goal to enter into a business relationship should not only be to make money — but to create opportunities for people. And people connect from the heart.

As you can imagine, everyone left Alan's negotiation super excited about the new venture we were about to launch.

No Asshole Rule

Just as important to Alan as finding a "win-win" in a negotiation is knowing the other party's values and beliefs before entering into a business relationship. As Alan says, you can never do a good deal with someone that doesn't have strong values. Alan likes to call this, the "No Asshole Rule."

The basics of this rule is that if you see that the person you are going to do business with — whether a client, an employee, a vendor, or a potential business partner — is an asshole, you should never do business with them. Even if the potential business is incredible. Alan believes we need to be happy and enjoy doing business. So, it's not worth getting involved with people that won't let us enjoy the work we do and support people.

During CURATED's early years, we faced significant challenges due to difficult clients who took advantage of us. Because we were new in our business, we didn't know how to set defined limits with our clients. So, some of them started to push us too hard to sell them cars at the cheapest price. They even renegotiated our service bills to the point we were losing money — and they were happy with that outcome.

Due to our inexperience in the industry, we thought these types of client relationships and expectations were normal. And since we had a limited client base at the time, we felt compelled to tolerate their behavior.

However, we failed to recognize the true cost of this situation — both in terms of financial impact and the toll it took on our team's energy and wellbeing. On days when we had to do these deals, our lives became miserable. These individuals drained us of precious time, resources, and energy, and prevented us from focusing on business growth and, ultimately, our happiness.

Becoming increasingly frustrated with this situation, we knew something had to give. So, we had a lengthy conversation with Alan. At that point, everything about how we approached our clients changed.

Alan introduced us to the concept of the "No Asshole Rule" and emphasized its importance in our future interactions. From that moment forward, we made the decision to implement this rule with everyone who had a relationship with CURATED: clients, employees, vendors, and business partners. The task was daunting — as it upended the way we were used to doing business — but John and I ultimately made the difficult choice to part ways with some clients. This decision was particularly nerve-wracking since these clients generated a significant portion of our revenue. So, losing them had the potential to put our company in a precarious situation.

But to our surprise, the exact opposite happened!

By embracing the No Asshole Rule, we completely transformed our business.

Instead of spending energy and losing money on negative clients, we were able to redirect our focus toward clients who genuinely appreciated and respected our work. Their satisfaction was so evident that they started referring more clients to us — and our company's reputation began to flourish within the industry. Over the years, we also had to apply the same rule to a few employees, and the overall energy within the company underwent a remarkable change.

As Alan wisely put it, even a single drop of wine in a glass of water can instantly alter its color. Or as John says now, "Moral compass is greater than any profit."

Transparency — The Truth, Be Yourself

Early in my career, I wasn't someone who easily showed my cards within business. I kept myself guarded. I worked from a persona of whom I thought a businessperson was. Up until this point in my life, nothing in my business experience showed me that any other way was possible. To me, vulnerability could be a weakness. And you never wanted to display your or your company's weaknesses.

Alan opened my eyes.

To Alan, the only way to negotiate or have a business conversation is to be transparent — and vulnerable.

In business and in life, Alan makes himself completely vulnerable. He opens himself up as a person and reveals the truths about his company. He tells the good and the bad. He shares the issues they face. And his deals and relationships always come out stronger as a result.

I've been in negotiations with Alan where he's upfront and honest about any struggles or challenges he or his company is facing. And I was always shocked. I used to say to him, "Alan, now they know everything! We have zero negotiation power! Why did you tell them that?!"

And his response was always, "No, Jordi. We need to be transparent. Otherwise, a year from now, we'll have even bigger issues down the road."

In business — especially during a negotiation — people tend to project a version of themselves that may not be reality. They fabricate an image of what they want the world to see. This could be by wearing expensive clothing and expensive watches. Or how they talk about themselves, their lifestyle, etc. During negotiations, they portray this perfect image of their company and themselves. They highlight all the amazing things while never revealing any struggles or challenges. It's not fully their fault. The traditional business model and mindsight doesn't teach you that exposing weaknesses and leaning into vulnerability can be a strength.

So while people think that only conveying an image of success is necessary for business, what they're really doing is shielding who they and their company truly are. Like the great Wizard in the Wizard of Oz, they're hiding the real person behind the curtain. And being dishonest in the process. And that misdirect can much more negatively affect someone's life or business than transparency and vulnerable leadership ever will.

Why?

Vulnerability is the main tenet of doing business from the heart. When you lead with vulnerability, you allow access to parts of you that you may typically close shut: You are honest about your emotions. You are open about life experiences that could be affecting you. You admit failures or weaknesses. You authentically communicate.

Since implementing this mindset at CURATED, I've seen that people really appreciate when someone is vulnerable and opens up. This transparency and access to who you and your company really are gives them space to feel comfortable opening up and sharing, too. They also better trust you. By acting this way, you create a stronger connection between both parties and the energy completely shifts into a true bond. Everytime you are vulnerable, you open a door for someone to realize who you are and how you feel, and change their behavior toward you.

You also improve your business results.

Companies that recognize the correlation

between trust and transparency, and take great action to improve those factors in their workplace, perform better. They're 2 times more likely to meet or exceed financial targets and 2.4 times more likely to engage employees with meaningful work.[24] Further, when leaders regularly show vulnerability, employees are 5.3 times more likely to trust them. And employees trust leaders 7.5 times more when they are honest about their own failures and shortcomings.[26]

One time at CURATED, we got into a slight financial quagmire where we had lots of cars sold but not paid for yet. On the other side, we had four cars coming from Japan that took longer than expected to get to the US. This situation put us in a super complicated cash-flow situation where I didn't even know if we were going to be able to cover our payroll that month. Keep in mind that the cars we buy today typically cost millions of dollars, and we must always pay in cash. Simply put, we were in a bad situation.

So, we decided to be transparent with one of our best clients whom we knew had money at hand. We called him and explained the situation we were in.

And we asked if he could help us by buying a car he'd been interested in but was being wishy-washy about. He wasn't 100% sure if he even wanted the car. So, we told him that if in 8 months he doesn't want the car, then we'd buy it back.

By doing so — making sure this situation was a win-win for both of us — he decided to help. As a result, we were able to meet our financial obligations and payroll. And everyone was happy. Plus, our client appreciated our honesty, vulnerability, and transparency with him. This deepened our relationship.

Years prior, we couldn't have imagined being so transparent to a client about a financial issue we were having. But, by prioritizing honesty and vulnerability, our client could see we were coming from the heart. And because he valued our relationship, he chose to help.

So, I encourage you to not be afraid to show the world who you really are.

You don't need to pretend to be someone else — or to portray a version of success for yourself or your company. Instead, lean into leading from vulnerability and transparency. Lead from the truth. And negotiate from the heart.

Once you do, I assure you, your heart will become your superpower!

HYPNOSIS MEDITATION

Believe, Behave, Become!
Scan this QR code for a guided hypnosis meditation.
This meditation will help you connect your brain
with your heart, allowing you to fully experience this
chapter's emotions. By doing so, you can embrace its
concepts and transform your behavior to align with
the person you aspire to become!

JOURNALING

**What is the image that you portray in
your business relationships?**

How close to your real self is it?

In what ways could you be more vulnerable in your personal and business life?

What effects could this vulnerability create?

Explore current negotiations you have and how you can better lead from the heart and embrace transparency.

9

COMMUNICATE AUTHENTICALLY

"It's important to have authentic conversations!"

When John and I started CURATED, communication wasn't our strong suit.

I was too direct and straightforward. John was too passive and soft. He hated conflict, which made direct conversation difficult. So, he tended to communicate in a shade of gray. He tiptoed around his thoughts to the point that the message the other person received was completely different from what he meant to share. Meanwhile, I didn't have patience for his communication style. I just wanted him to get to the point and tell me how he felt!

As a result, conflict and confrontation would emerge between us — and hit up against our egos.

So, John put up walls and avoided telling me how he was feeling. And I became too aggressive and allowed rage to kick in. This dynamic made our communication as partners very difficult. Had we maintained this friction, we would've threatened the very foundation of our relationship and our business.

Unfortunately, many people spend their lives operating within this space. They become afraid of hurting the person's feelings. Afraid of their reactions. Afraid how someone might interpret their words. Afraid of what the person may say about them afterward. Afraid of judgment. Afraid of difficulty. And we let this fear and worry drive us and completely absorb our ability to communicate what we need to say.

Or, perhaps they do the opposite: They lead with ego. That they're always right. That their voices matter more than the other person's. So they don't let others talk. They talk over people. They don't listen. They chastise and threaten.

In the process, these dynamics ruin relationships. Jeopardize careers. Deflate self-esteems. And we can bottle up all these emotions, which further threatens our health and wellbeing. Resentment and passive aggressiveness then emerge and dominate how we communicate.

By doing so, we become the exact opposite of authentic to our emotions. We become a shell of our voice.

At some point, Alan realized that John and I were having challenges communicating. And he brought up the concept of how important it was to have authentic conversation. He guided us on being direct and transparent while always speaking from the heart. We also saw this communication style in action through the way he talked with us. Alan always shared his honest feelings and opinions, and did so from a constructive perspective. Rather than let ego or insecurity lead the way, he allowed his heart to guide him. And he talked with true care for us and gave space to share our voices in return.

Over time, John and I started to communicate authentically. The shift required us to let down our walls and lead with empathy. Rather than see the space between us a potential threat, we leaned into the beauty of being vulnerable and honest with one another. Of using our heart. We knew that neither of us ever intended to hurt the other person. We also knew that we shared the same vision and values for what we wanted out of our company: to honor the history and value of the cars we sold while positively impacting and changing people's lives for the better.

So, we embraced our trust in each other and let our hearts do the talking instead of our minds. Once we did, everything changed. Our relationship as business partners became unbreakable. We both knew that we had each other's back and love for something bigger — this deepened our bond and united us as brothers.

And we were able to build a foundation of communicating authentically across everything we do at CURATED.

"Underpromise and Overdeliver"

Before meeting Alan, I'd never heard of the premise to underpromise on something and then overdeliver.

To Alan, this tenet is one of his key factors for success. He believes you should always strive to deliver more than you promised, whether for an employee, a client, a vendor, or any company stakeholder. If you do the opposite — overpromise and underdeliver — you'll create missed goals and unrealistic expectations. This outcome generates frustration, anger, and resentment for everyone involved.

When John and I were creating our first business plans to raise money from investors, we thought we were conveying these lofty goals that would inspire people. Alan, however, wasn't convinced. He was always telling us we were being too optimistic. Instead, he felt we should be more conservative. Then, we could overdeliver and surprise our investors with good news. He believed we should do this even if it meant we got a lower valuation for our company. He also believed it wasn't worth the stress our optimism would create for us to accomplish those goals if a lower number was also acceptable.

So, we had to both dream big — while being realistic about what we could do in the moment to reach our dreams. By managing expectations in this way, you can create a more tangible plan of action that you're more capable of achieving.

Managing this principle with clients is especially important. If you create lofty expectations for what you can deliver to them, and you don't meet them, they'll become frustrated. And a frustrated client is a lost client. On the flip side, if you exceed your clients' expectations, you'll create a client and a referral partner for life who'll talk about you to all their friends and colleagues.

Similarly, setting unrealistic expectations for employees that they can't meet can be detrimental to their performance and happiness. Employees who can't fulfill the goals you set for them become stressed and disengaged.[27] They also can resort to unethical behavior like lying to clients or customers (due to trying to meet the lofty expectations you put on them).[28] And once behaviors like lying kick in, authentic communication completely shuts down.

And this environment can create a toxic work environment that affects your bottom line — poor communication and lack of transparency are key drivers.[29] In fact, US companies who communicate poorly collectively have up to $1.2 trillion in productivity losses every year.[30] Imagine what those companies could do with that money to benefit their employees and their communities had they not let communication drag them down! When communication is poor, employees become unhappy. They don't feel appreciated and start to withdraw from their role. They even become reluctant to innovate for the company. As a result, they doubt their abilities and, eventually, the entire company — threatening productivity and the bottom line.[31] Consequently, 20% of employees have left a company due to its toxic environment and 35% will take a pay cut to work somewhere that isn't toxic.[32]

Think about that for a minute!

People are willing to make less money in order to avoid the stress of a toxic environment. And how sad this reality is! Since employees find much of their life purpose through their work, we should be doing everything we can to ensure that our employees feel valued, respected, and heard. We should be creating a culture that people want to be part of — that inspires them to be their best selves. We should be paying them their worth and creating an environment that prioritizes their happiness!

So to communicate authentically, you also need to be realistic about goals setting and how you manage others' expectations. Communicate from a place of honesty. Be grounded about what employees can achieve and what you can realistically deliver to clients, partners, and any stakeholders. And be transparent about the reasons for those expectations.

And then, exceed them!

Talk With Your Heart

Today at CURATED, our first core value is: Use

Your Heart.

To us, this tenet means that we must genuinely care for all company stakeholders — employees, partners, vendors, clients. We must also love the journey and drive with passion and optimism.

Because of this value, we prioritize talking with your heart and not your mind. As a result, any manager that is having a conversation does so by speaking with their heart. Through this, communicating authentically becomes easy, because you don't allow ego or fear to drive the conversation. You respect the person that you're talking with and look directly at them. Instead of putting up walls, you let your guards down. You remove any filters that you used to protect yourself. You create an even playing field where you own up to mistakes and learn from one another. And you don't tiptoe around details. You are caring, honest, and forthcoming.

In this manner, you're able to look into someone's eyes and tell them what you think with complete transparency and warmth.

A Savvy Professional Who Was Used to Pushing Hard

One of our managers is an extremely skilled and experienced employee who joined our company after moving from New York City. So, he had that New York style of pushing hard, expressing himself with short sentences, and going straight to the point. While his heart was in the right place, he didn't know how to use his heart in the business world.

Not long after we hired him, I saw a couple red flags emerge from his behavior. The first was an email response he had to a team member that was bringing to him an opportunity, and in response, he delivered back a short, almost terse, direct question. The tone was abrupt and almost dismissive, and not at all in the style of how we communicate at CURATED. The second flag was during a weekly management team meeting where I saw his ego kick in as he got defensive when the team questioned him about something. Again, not a way that we interact with one another.

John and I knew that we had to address these red flags before they got worse. So, we had an authentic, heartfelt conversation with him to share what we'd seen in his actions — and why they weren't a culture fit at CURATED. We told him how we knew his heart was in the right place, but he had to open his heart and express love in every communication. Rather than being short and direct in this tone through email, he had to lead with warmth and excitement for the employee. We said, "If it was your daughter that you sent that message to, would you have answered her the way you did in your email?" Once he processed this information and thought

about the question, his face changed
completely. He said, "Definitely, no!!"
Then, we talked about the importance
of vulnerability and how no one on the
team is here to attack him, no reason
to get defensive. And he confessed
that he'd never worked anywhere that
communicated with and led from the
heart — so he'd never seen this in action.
He understood now why it mattered and
was ready to change.

Immediately, he made a massive shift
in how he communicated and left his ego
at the door. And he began talking with
the heart. All from a 30-minute authentic
conversation.

To ensure we support this belief at CURATED, we've ingrained open communication into our meetings. We structure them in a way where everyone has a space to share and express their opinions — from the cleaning person to John. No hierarchy exists in who's allowed to have a voice or when. We're all equals. We also have integrated the People Analyzer, a tool that bases conversations around employee performance on their alignment with our core values. Rather than lead with the mind, we lead from the heart (our values) — and this method has opened up our ability to have candid, genuine discussions.

One quarterly management meeting, we had a beautiful moment between John and me. During meetings, our team gives shout-outs to one another to recognize gratitude for something that person did. One thing that can be a challenge for John is staying organized. As a result, he often wasn't attending our meetings — and we'd had to reschedule meetings to make sure he could attend. So, I'd privately shared with John how important I believed it was that he attended meetings with us. And he took this to heart and began to attend each session. So this one specific morning, I gave a shout-out to John for his commitment to our meetings. And then, John said, "A shout-out to you, Jordi, for helping me realize how important it was that I attend meetings." And we had this wonderful moment of thanks between us, shared with our employees.

And then, a ripple effect occurred.

Another employee gave a shout-out for the fact we organized these meetings. They also gave a shout-out for starting meetings with meditations.[4] And then, one after another, shout-outs kept happening. And John and I were just sitting back and watching all of this magic occur on its own! At the meeting's end, another employee gave a shout-out to John and I that this amazing environment was happening because of us. They were thankful that we empowered them

---

4 I began meditating in 2020 and saw a powerful shift in my mindfulness. So, I now meditate every morning. But for a while, I kept this part of myself hidden from my employees. I was worried they would judge me for meditating. Eventually, I realized I had to authentically be me and stop worrying. Then, one powerful moment happened in July 2024 when I woke up, went for a run, and started meditating. During my mediation, employees started popping up in my mind, and I connected with every one of them. I felt so grateful and had so much love for them.

The next Monday morning, our life coach was unable to attend our scheduled session with the group. So, I had to figure out what to do in her place. I decided to focus on meditation. In our meeting, I asked everyone, "Who meditates on a weekly basis?" And I told them about what had happened to me after my run that morning and how each one of them came to my meditation individually and that I had felt so much love and gratefulness for them. I said, "Thank you so much!" to them. Instantly, their faces changed completely! They were wow'd and amazed that their boss could be so vulnerable. And our bonds deepened. Now, we start our Monday mornings with meditations, and employees even lead us in the sessions.

to do their jobs through the company's values and supporting their higher purpose.

John and I were so amazed and thankful for this authentic moment to exist. And it completely happened on its own because we created a space where employees have a voice! And it saddens me that every company doesn't have experiences like this with their employees and partners.

So, my friends, this is what communicating from the heart can do for you, for your employees, and for your company. You create an environment of honesty and respect supported by realistic expectations. Of thankfulness and appreciation. Of true warmth, camaraderie, and concern for one another.

In short, you create a bond that's unbreakable. As one of our employees has put it, "The people here and how we want others to be treated, we're family."

And now you, dear readers, are part of this family, too!

HYPNOSIS MEDITATION 

Believe, Behave, Become!
Scan this QR code for a guided hypnosis meditation.
This meditation will help you connect your brain
with your heart, allowing you to fully experience this
chapter's emotions. By doing so, you can embrace its
concepts and transform your behavior to align with
the person you aspire to become!

JOURNALING

**What's a conversation that feels difficult
or heavy that you need to have?**

Explore how you truly feel and make a list of all the emotions you feel about this situation.

Identify how you can better have this conversation by leading from the heart.

Once you're ready for the conversation, come from a place of vulnerability: Show them how you feel and be honest about the emotions you have. Approach everything from the heart.

10

SAY, I LOVE YOU

"You know I love you?"

o the people in your life know that you love and care for them? Think about this question!

I never used to tell anyone, "I love you." Not even my family members. Maybe this was partly cultural, but I didn't grow up so easily expressing my emotions in this way. And I often hid how I felt, especially in professional settings. Business was for business, not for your emotions. I bottled my feelings up and sealed them shut. No one needed to see that side of me.

So, the first time I heard Alan tell me, "I love you," it was jarring. And liberating! I felt special!

Someone that I deeply respect just said he loved me.

Instantly, Alan defied the norms of my business relationships. He showed me the power of love, urging me to open my heart to those around me. He taught me the value of vulnerability and the profound impact of openly expressing love and care. And that, by doing so, you open yourself, others, and your business up to even greater heights.

And since knowing him, I've realized that Alan's truly exceptional quality and core value is his belief in and embrace of unconditional love. From this tenet, he makes every decision in his life.

In fact, Alan infuses every interaction with love. And he doesn't confine his love to mere words — he demonstrates it through his actions. He exemplifies love in every encounter, leaving a lasting impact on all those around him. Whether it's a kind gesture, a listening ear, or a heartfelt compliment, his expressions of love are tangible and genuine.

It's from this mindset that the amazing LAZ Hugs were born!

And it doesn't matter who they are or what role a

person serves at LAZ. Alan shows everyone he loves them. His love knows no bounds, which he extends to every single person. His secret to doing so is simple yet profound: Fill our minds with thoughts of love, forgiveness, and compassion. From this place, we tap into an infinite wellspring of love that nourishes our relationships and transforms our lives.

Time and again, Alan shares his joy in spending time with me and those around him, exclaiming, "Do you know how happy I am to be here with you?" And every time he shares that with me, he reaffirms that I am loved, appreciated, and undeniably special. And our bond deepens, and my appreciation and respect for him grows. And I instantly feel good about myself and want to share this positivity and warmth with others.

So, this is where the traditional way of doing business has failed us — love has been left out of the equation.

To this point, Alan has said, "People aren't used to capitalism and love." And he's right! How often have you heard your supervisors or even your colleagues tell you that they love you? How often have you told vendors or business partners that you appreciate them? How often have you made business decisions from a place of love?

Chances are, the answer is, *Rarely!* Maybe even, *never.* And if so, that's okay! It's not entirely your fault.

Even a Google search for "capitalism and love" brings up results focused on how companies can profit off of love and relationships. Or, how you can navigate romantic relationships in the workplace.

But, love is such a far-reaching, complex, and human emotion! It's so important to the human experience that many cultures (and thereby languages) have various words and definitions of love. For example, Tamil (spoken in South Asia) has about 50 words for love. Spanish has about four. Japanese has three. Sanskrit has over 200!

So, if love is so deeply part of the human condition and consciousness, why are we not infusing our companies and life with it?

Just look around and think of how capitalism

could be different if we always came from a place of love: *Would employees work 8 hours a day and still struggle to pay their bills? Would business models contribute to deforestation and species extinction? Would child labor still exist in supply chains?*

Doing business from a place of love leaves no room for people to focus solely on making a profit at the expense of others. Because when you lead with love, you put humanity and empathy first. You care about others' wellbeing outside of your own, with no expectations in return. You enhance positivity. You communicate from the heart.

That's what unconditional love is about!

Make Kindness Your M.O.

Expressing love is way more than just a word and saying "I love you."

When you do business from a place of expressing love, it becomes a constant in your day-to-day activity. Doing so can mean, saying good morning and offering a hug. Or giving a high five when someone's done a great job (or even, just because you want to). Maybe, you simply take time to ask how someone is feeling — and give them time to express themselves and genuinely listen. Maybe, you reach out to a colleague who you know is stressed and simply let them know you're there for them in case they need anything.

Love is a frequency that you tune up to, and once you're there, you don't focus on the negative. So, you stop judging people for their mistakes. If an employee or a vendor accidentally messes up, rather than blame and shame them, lean into helping make the situation better! You give them opportunities to grow. You support them and make sure they feel supported in return.

Acts of love don't have to always be grand gestures. Often, the smallest acts can have the greatest impact. And you infuse this sense of being into every relationship you have and every business decision you make.

Here at CURATED, leading with unconditional love has become simply who we are — we live this value every day.

Once, when Alan and I were communicating with

some business partners, I was frequently receiving emails from one of the accountants. And this woman was just downright mean to me. In every email she sent she demeaned me, talked down to me, belittled me. And with every email, I got angrier and angrier — until I hit a breaking point. I told Alan, "I can't take this anymore! She's making my life miserable." And I wanted to rage my anger at her so she felt as miserable as I felt. Alan's response, however, was, "Jordi, that's not the way. You need to kill her with kindness. Show her how to lead with love. You'll turn your foe into a friend."

Leading with love was the absolute last way I wanted to interact with this lady!

But, I listened to Alan and challenged myself. And the first email draft I wrote, I reviewed it and thought, *She doesn't deserve these nice words at all!! I don't want to send them to her!* I sent the email anyway. And I did the same thing with the next email and the next email. And sure enough, I was able to release all of the anger I was holding inside. And rather than dreading my communications with her, I began to feel a sense of calm. By reclaiming our interactions with love, I no longer allowed her negativity to control my sense of wellbeing. And I was more peaceful in my business interactions overall.

Leading with love has even meant that we've helped some of our competitors become successful within our industry! Rather than be cut throat, we've fostered growth and made introductions. We all have room to be successful. So why not lead with love and foster opportunities for everyone?

Remember how at CURATED we now start Monday meetings with sharing gratitude toward something someone has done? We designed our meetings this way specifically to open up everyone's ability to feel and share love with one another! And to start the week off with such positive vibes! And it's working — the energy everyone feels after these gratitude moments is invigorating and contagious.

And, science backs this up: it's called the Emotional Contagion, when one person mimics another person's emotions or actions. We can pass our emotions on — and reflect them from others —

without even knowing that we are, be them excited, happy, angry, or sad (or otherwise). And you can even mimic someone quicker than you can catch a cold![33]

So think about that for a second: Every time you've been frustrated or angry — and you've responded with this frustration and anger to another — the other person is possibly mimicking these emotions, perhaps without even realizing it. And applying these feelings to their own lives. And anyone they come in contact with can then also catch this negativity and anger, and continue passing it on.

And this is exactly what the soul of this book is about: pay it forward.

Every single day, you have a choice to lead with unconditional love. You have the choice to prioritize humanity and compassion. You have the choice to generate positive vibes that are going to affect other people in your life — that they, in turn, will mimic, and pass on to others. Be it colleagues, employees, vendors, friends, their family, and so on.

And this ripple effect can then cast itself far beyond those people and swell into their communities. And if you've led with love, if you've chosen to say I love you through your actions and words, think of how much positivity we're all paying forward together!

So, dear reader, I ask you to consider the depth of your relationships. Reflect on the power of expressing love and care openly. Look into the eyes of your loved ones, friends, and colleagues, and let them know how much they mean to you. Embrace vulnerability, and extend a hand of support. Be transparent in your actions and honest with your voice. And lead from the heart. For it is in these small yet profound acts that we can transform lives and create a world infused with compassion, empathy, and understanding.

By doing so, we're able to transform business through unconditional love. And this, my friends, is the only way that we and everything around us can truly shine. What a beautiful world that will be!

HYPNOSIS MEDITATION 

Believe, Behave, Become!

Scan this QR code for a guided hypnosis meditation. This meditation will help you connect your brain with your heart, allowing you to fully experience this chapter's emotions. By doing so, you can embrace its concepts and transform your behavior to align with the person you aspire to become!

JOURNALING

When was the last time you told a family member I love you? a friend? a colleague at work?

In what ways do you currently express love?

In what ways can you better express "I Love You" to people in your life?

Have you ever made a business decision from a place of love?

Reflect on how you can apply this approach to your business life.

EPILOGUE

"We are the kind of
people that never,
ever give up."

Early in my relationship with Alan, he gave me a bracelet that said, "Never, ever give up."

I wore this bracelet for years — and it became sort of a lifeline for me. Whenever I would feel overwhelmed or dragged down, I'd look at this bracelet and instantly find my motivation! It inspired me to continue chasing my dreams, to keep believing in myself, to never stop, no matter what obstacles life would throw at me.

As an immigrant who at one point had only $150 in my bank account, I'm humbled in all I've achieved. This journey has been one of the biggest roller coasters of my life, filled with ups and downs. At times, I felt that my American dream was about to end, and I would have to accept defeat. However, the universe had more to offer me!

Throughout this experience, I ended up discovering that when you're a good person and focus on helping others, a helping hand is always ready to support you. So now, I want to extend this support to you: My dear friends, no matter what you want to achieve in life — never, ever give up.

Whether you come from a poor family or you didn't go to college or you don't speak the language of the country you're in — whatever your situation — everything is possible! You just need to believe in yourself and go for it! Lots of good people will come along the way ready to give you a hand when you most need it.

So, remember…

Set your goals.

Dream big, and surrender to life.

Live in the present!

Communicate with love.

And most importantly, use your heart!

Apply the principles from this book and focus on making an impact on your community. The rest will come naturally. While my guidance requires time to practice and integrate into your daily life, it's all possible! As I've seen firsthand, the results of infusing unconditional love into business are incredible.

From there, remember to pay it forward! Share this book with others, offer them your heart, help them without expecting anything in return. And then, encourage them to pay it forward, too! These ripple effects are what connect us all — and can invigorate the way we live each day and put energy into the world.

Together, we can transform humanity where we all create conscious businesses infused with unconditional love that lead with caring for our people, our communities, and this beautiful planet we live in!

Pay It Forward to someone else by scanning this code!

HYPNOSIS MEDITATION 

Believe, Behave, Become!

Scan this QR code for a guided hypnosis meditation.
This meditation will help you connect your brain
with your heart, allowing you to fully experience this
chapter's emotions. By doing so, you can embrace its
concepts and transform your behavior to align with
the person you aspire to become!

JOURNALING

ENDNOTES

1   Vaish, A., Grossmann, T., & Woodward, A. "Not all emotions are created equal: The negativity bias in social-emotional development," *Psychological Bulletin*, 134(3) (2008): 383–403. https://doi.org/10.1037/0033-2909.134.3.383.

2   Matthew Solan, "Thoughts on optimism," *Harvard Health Publishing*, 2021, https://www.health.harvard.edu/mind-and-mood/thoughts-on-optimism.

    Mark Murphy, "Optimistic Employees Are 103% More Inspired To Give Their Best Effort At Work, New Data Reveals," *Forbes*, 2020, https://www.forbes.com/sites/markmurphy/2020/02/26/optimistic-employees-are-103-more-inspired-to-give-their-best-effort-at-work-new-data-reveals/.

3   Niamh Delmar, "Here's Why Smiling Is Good
     For Your Health, According To A Psychologist,"
     RTE, 2023, https://www.rte.ie/lifestyle/liv-
     ing/2023/0608/1388049-heres-why-smiling-is-good-
     for-your-health/.

4   Frances McGlone & Susannah Walker, "Four Ways
     Hugs Are Good For Your Health," *Greater Good
     Magazine,* June 22, 2021, https://greatergood.
     berkeley.edu/article/item/four_ways_hugs_are_
     good_for_your_health.

5   Michael Cardman, "'Respectful Treatment' Biggest
     Driver Of Job Satisfaction, Says SHRM Survey,"
     BrightMine, April 24, 2017, https://hrcenter.
     us.brightmine.com/news/respectful-treatment-
     biggest-driver-of-job-satisfaction-says-shrm-sur-
     vey/25345/.

6   Avraham Kluger and Guy Itzchakov, "The
     Power of Listening at Work," *Annual Review of
     Organizational Psychology and Organizational
     Behavior,* 9, 2022, https://www.researchgate.net/
     publication/353573217_The_Power_of_Listening_
     at_Work.

7   Janetta Lun et al, "On Feeling Understood and
     Feeling Well: The Role of Interdependence," *Journal
     of research in personality,* vol. 42,6, 2008, 1623-1628.

doi:10.1016/j.jrp.2008.06.009, https://www.ncbi.
nlm.nih.gov/pmc/articles/PMC2652476/.

8   David Scott Yeager et al, "Breaking the cycle of
     mistrust: Wise interventions to provide critical
     feedback across the racial divide," *Journal of
     Experimental Psychology*, 143, no. 2, 2014,
     https://www.apa.org/pubs/journals/releases/xge-
     a0033906.pdf.

9   "Mission and Vision," Conscious Capitalism,
     accessed September 3, 2024, https://www.con-
     sciouscapitalism.org/mission-and-vision.

     Jeff Fromm and Jeff King, "Only Conscious
     Capitalists Will Survive," *Forbes*, December
     4, 2013, https://www.forbes.com/sites/
     onmarketing/2013/12/04/only-conscious-capital-
     ists-will-survive/.

10   Jessica Cerretani, "The Contagion of Happiness:
     Harvard researchers are discovering how we can
     all get happy," *Harvard Medicine*, 2011, https://
     magazine.hms.harvard.edu/articles/contagion-hap-
     piness.

11   UKG, "A Silenced Workforce: Four in Five
     Employees Feel Colleagues Aren't Heard Equally,
     Says Research from The Workforce Institute at
     UKG," June 22, 2021, https://www.ukg.com/

about-us/newsroom/silenced-workforce-four-five-em-
ployees-feel-colleagues-arent-heard-equally-says.

12   Perceptyx, "From Insight to Action: New Data on
     the State of Employee Listening," April 12, 2024,
     https://blog.perceptyx.com/from-insight-to-action-
     new-data-on-the-state-of-employee-listening.

13   Naina Dhingra, Andrew Samo, Bill Schaninger,
     and Matt Schrimper, "Help your employees find
     purpose—or watch them leave," *McKinsey*, April 5,
     2021, https://www.mckinsey.com/capabilities/peo-
     ple-and-organizational-performance/our-insights/
     help-your-employees-find-purpose-or-watch-them-
     leave#/.

14   Marcus Buckingham, "80% of employees only care
     about their paychecks—here's how to beat anxiety
     (and actually enjoy work)," *Yahoo!Finance,* March 4,
     2019, https://finance.yahoo.com/news/80-employ-
     ees-only-care-paychecks-180706049.html.

15   "How Liking Your Job Will Help You Succeed,"
     University of Southern California, accessed
     September 3, 2024, https://appliedpsychologydegree.
     usc.edu/blog/how-liking-your-job-will-help-you-suc-
     ceed.

16   Jenny Fernandez, Kathryn Landis, and Julie Lee,
     "Helping Gen Z Employees Find Their Place at

Work," *Harvard Business Review,* January 18, 2023, https://hbr.org/2023/01/helping-gen-z-employees-find-their-place-at-work.

17 Jack Zenger and Joseph Folkman, "Do You Tell Your Employees You Appreciate Them?" *Harvard Business Review*, September 12, 2022, https://hbr.org/2022/09/do-you-tell-your-employees-you-appreciate-them.

18 Christopher "CJ" Gross, "A Better Approach to Mentorship," *Harvard Business Review,* June 6, 2023, https://hbr.org/2023/06/a-better-approach-to-mentorship.

19 Kate Den Houter and Ellyn Maese, "Mentors and Sponsors Make the Difference," *Gallup*, April 13, 2023, https://www.gallup.com/workplace/473999/mentors-sponsors-difference.aspx.

20 Teresa M. Amabile and Steven J. Kramer, "The Power of Small Wins," *Harvard Business Review*, May 2011, https://hbr.org/2011/05/the-power-of-small-wins?registration=success.

21 David Villa, "How Celebrating Success Can Lead to More Of It," *Forbes*, May 12, 2022, https://www.forbes.com/councils/forbesagencycoun-

cil/2022/05/12/how-celebrating-success-can-lead-to-more-of-it/.

22 Jeff Fromm and Jeff King, "Only Conscious Capitalists Will Survive," *Forbes*, December 4, 2013, https://www.forbes.com/sites/onmarketing/2013/12/04/only-conscious-capitalists-will-survive/.

23 Jump Associates, "The Payback on Purpose: How Purpose-Driven Companies Outperform the Competition," 2023, https://www.jumpassociates.com/wp-content/uploads/2023/10/Jump-The-Payback-on-Purpose-Oct-2023.pdf

24 Alison Wood Brooks, "Emotion and the Art of Negotiation: How to use your feelings to your advantage," *Harvard Business Review*, December 2015, https://hbr.org/2015/12/emotion-and-the-art-of-negotiation.

25 Jason Flynn et al, "The transparency paradox: Could less be more when it comes to trust?" *Deloitte Insights*, February 5, 2024, https://www2.deloitte.com/us/en/insights/focus/human-capital-trends/2024/transparency-in-the-workplace.html.

26 Richmond Fourmy, "Why Executives Need to Practice Vulnerable Leadership—And How To Do

It," *DDI*, August 24, 2023, https://www.ddiworld.
com/blog/vulnerable-leadership.

27   Gallup, "2024 Report: State of the Global
Workforce—The Voice Of The World's Employees,"
2024.

28   Dina Gerdeman, "When Managers Set Unrealistic
Expectations, Employees Cut Ethical Corners,"
Harvard Business Review, April 30, 2024, https://
hbswk.hbs.edu/item/when-managers-set-unrealis-
tic-expectations-employees-cut-ethical-corners.

29   Melissa Russell, "How to Build—and Improve—
Company Culture," *Harvard Professional and
Executive Development*, June 26, 2024, https://pro-
fessional.dce.harvard.edu/blog/how-to-build-and-
improve-company-culture/.

30   Grammarly, "The High Stakes," *Atlantic Re:think*,
2024, https://www.theatlantic.com/sponsored/
grammarly-2024/the-high-stakes-of-poor-communi-
cation/3877/

31   Noviana Rismawati, Dewi Nafiati, Tomi Azami,
and Neni Hendaryati, "Cooperative Learning:
Alternatif Untuk Meningkatkan Communication
Skill Pada Sekolah Boarding," Jurnal Pendidikan
Ekonomi (JURKAMI). 9. 538-553. 10.31932/jpe.
v9i2.3656, 2024, https://www.researchgate.net/

publication/375903142_Communication_Barriers_
in_Work_Environment_Understanding_Impact_
and_Challenges.

32   Aoibhinn McBride, "Toxic Work Culture Is Driving
     Away 1 in 5 Employees," *The Hill*, May 3, 2024,
     https://thehill.com/lobbying/4638592-toxic-work-
     culture-is-driving-away-1-in-5-employees/https:/
     www.intoo.com/us/blog/combating-workplace-tox-
     icity/.

33   Jodi Schulz, "Emotions Are Contagious: Learn
     What Science and Research Has to Say About It,"
     Michigan State University Extension, August 16,
     2017, https://www.canr.msu.edu/news/emotions_
     are_contagious_learn_what_science_and_research_
     has_to_say_about_it.